QUANTITATIVE CONSTRUCTION MANAGEMENT: USES OF LINEAR OPTIMIZATION
Robert M. Stark and Robert H. Mayer, Jr.

QUANTITATIVE CONSTRUCTION MANAGEMENT

QUANTITATIVE CONSTRUCTION MANAGEMENT

Uses of Linear Optimization

ROBERT M. STARK
ROBERT H. MAYER, JR.

A Wiley-Interscience Publication

JOHN WILEY & SONS

New York · Chichester · Brisbane · Toronto · Singapore

Library of Congress Cataloging in Publication Data:

Stark, Robert M., 1930–
  Quantitative construction management.

  (Construction management and engineering, ISSN 0193–9750)
  "A Wiley-Interscience publication."
  Bibliography: p.
  Includes index.
  1. Building—Mathematical models. 2. Construction
industry—Management—Mathematical models. 3. Linear
programming. I. Mayer, Robert H., Jr. II. Title.
III. Series.

TH153.S82 1983   624'.068   83-6907
ISBN 0-471-86959-7

Printed in the United States of America

10 9 8 7 6 5 4 3 2 1

SERIES PREFACE

Industry observers agree that most construction practitioners do not fully exploit the state of the art. We concur in this general observation. Further, we have acted by directing this series of works on Construction Management and Engineering to the continuing education and reference needs of today's practitioners.

Our design is inspired by the burgeoning technologies of systems engineering, modern management, information systems, and industrial engineering. We believe that the latest developments in these areas will serve to close the state of the art gap if they are astutely considered by management and knowledgeably applied in operations with personnel, equipment, and materials.

When considering the pressures and constraints of the world economic environment, we recognize an increasing trend toward large-scale operations and greater complexity in the construction product. To improve productivity and maintain acceptable performance standards, today's construction practitioner must broaden his concept of innovation and seek to achieve excellence through knowledgeable utilization of the resources. Therefore our focus is on skills and disciplines that support productivity, quality, and optimization in all aspects of the total facility acquisition process and at all levels of the management hierarchy.

We distinctly believe our perspective to be aligned with current trends and changes that portend the future of the construction industry. The books in this series should serve particularly well as textbooks at the graduate and senior undergraduate levels in a university construction curriculum or continuing education program.

JOHN F. PEEL BRAHTZ

La Jolla, California
February 1977

PREFACE

Managers expect the effectiveness with which tasks are performed to increase with experience and "know how." Typically, improvements are incremental, the limits of the current technology having been reached years earlier.

Occasionally, a newer technology becomes available that has the potential of accomplishing tasks with significantly greater effectiveness than would have been possible within the limits of the former technology. After a brief warm-up period, during which the capabilities of the newer technology are mastered, improvements sometimes are dramatic.

Linear optimization, or *linear programming* as it is more popularly known, is an example of such a new technology. Developed in the 1950s, *LP* (as it is also known) was intensively studied through the 1960s. Significant advances were made in mathematical theory, computational algorithms, and practical applications. Linear programming emerged in the 1970s as an important management tool. Indeed, from a survey of computer usage several years ago, IBM estimated that fully one-quarter of technical computation in the United States involved linear optimization. In the public sector, the military, and industry, linear programming is used by managers to aid their decisions ranging from the formulation of hospital menus to the setting up of production lines at General Motors. A 1979 issue of *INTERFACES,* a publication of the Institute of Management Sciences, reported that more than three-quarters of the larger industrial corporations responding to a survey had utilized linear programming.

The importance of linear programming stems from a fortuitous combination of factors, including the following:

1. It has a versatile mathematical format for a large variety of practical problems.
2. It can be effectively applied with virtually no understanding of the mathematical theory.
3. Solutions by automated computation are both readily obtainable and inexpensive.

Since the material in this book evolved (indeed, since it was set on these pages), personal microcomputers have gained an astonishing public acceptance. LP software package development surely will expand with continued industry usage. As with any technology, there are also limitations, and skill is required for best results. The text will clarify and expand upon these factors.

Linear programming is not entirely new to the construction industry. Critical path methods, which derive from linear programming, have been popular since the 1950s. In the early sixties, linear programming was used to determine economical blends of natural earth deposits to meet contract specifications. Nonetheless, linear programming doesn't have the prominent role in construction that it has in other industries. While there are literally hundreds of papers and many dozens of books on linear programming and its applications, relatively little relates to construction management. To our knowledge, this volume is the first to deal exclusively with this subject.

A feature of this book is that virtually every chapter deals with a construction management problem of everyday interest and formulates it as a problem of linear optimization. The examples have been limited to actual, or at least credible, construction management uses of linear programming. They span many construction management tasks: from capital budgeting, contract selection and bidding, project planning and scheduling, to resource utilization. Sometimes conventional methods are described for comparison with linear optimization methods. While the majority of examples relate to horizontal construction, our intent is to illustrate and suggest uses of linear programming that readers can extend to other types of construction management.

An effort has been made to keep the book both readable and self-contained. While there are no magical claims or "get rich quick" formulas, there are aids to mastering this new mathematical technology and its application.

Finally, it is a pleasure to acknowledge the help of colleagues and friends over long periods. Those most directly associated with this volume include John F. Peel Brahtz and Everett Smethurst among others representing John Wiley & Sons; the typing skills of Diane Iffland; and the support of the Office of Naval Research.

R. M. Stark
R. H. Mayer, Jr.

One Fox Lane
Newark, Delaware 19711
June 1983

CONTENTS

A firm can invest its limited assets in some projects chosen
from among many possibilities. Decisions on which projects to
choose for a maximum return (consistent with limitations on
machines, materials, personnel, and money) are guided by an
integer linear optimization.

Unbalancing a bid is usually a necessary part of every tender.
This chapter develops a method of computer-aided unbalancing
for large and long-term unit price proposals. For given project
information, the results cannot be improved upon.

Linear optimization is widely used to solve network problems.
Well-known critical path methods are one example, and cost ver-
sus time trade-offs are another.

QUANTITATIVE CONSTRUCTION MANAGEMENT

CHAPTER 1

QUARRYING WITH LINEAR PROGRAMMING

Rollin Along, a major road builder, needs these quantities of stones:

400 tons of Softa stone
500 tons of Harda stone
180 tons of Common stone

The required stones can be obtained from two quarries operated by Rollin Along. A single day of operation at the first quarry typically produces 160 tons of aggregate which, when processed and separated, yields 80, 60, and 20 tons of Softa, Harda, and Common stones, respectively. The second quarry can produce 180 tons daily, yielding 40, 80, and 60 tons of the respective types of stone.

Rollin Along regularly employs a single quarry crew. Since there is an imminent need for the stones, it is impractical to hire and train additional crews. Therefore, both quarries cannot be operated simultaneously. Management wants to know how to best schedule the single available quarry crew so as to obtain the needed stone as soon as possible.

One approach to a solution is to consider various schedules of working days in each quarry; enumerate the quantities of stone obtained with each schedule; and, finally, choose the schedule that yields the required stones in the least time. For example, Rollin Along could operate the second quarry alone for 10 days, or the first quarry alone for 9 days, or each quarry for 4 days. These are only three of many possible ways to schedule the quarry crew to obtain the required stone (and none of these is necessarily the best).

In principle, this trial and error approach is correct and could be used here. However, if there were many types of stone and many quarries, the number of schedule possibilities could become extremely large and their enumeration impractical. Let's try another approach.

Two decisions are required: the number of days to operate the first quarry (a variable denoted by X_1) and the number of days to operate the second quarry (denoted by X_2).* The total quarrying time (denoted by Z) can be written:

$$Z = X_1 + X_2$$

Since Rollin Along wants Z to be as small as possible, values of the *decision variables* X_1 and X_2 are sought which minimize this *objective equation*. One obvious solution that minimizes Z is to have $X_1 = X_2 = 0$; but with no quarrying there can be no stone. Clearly, the selected values of X_1 and X_2 must not only minimize Z, but they must yield the required quantities of stone. These requirements for stone are expressed by mathematical relationships called *constraints*.

Operating the first quarry for X_1 days would yield $80X_1$ (80 multiplied by X_1) tons of Softa stone, while X_2 days at the second quarry would yield $40X_2$ tons of Softa stone. The total yield of Softa stone would be $80X_1 + 40X_2$, and it must equal at least 400 tons. Therefore, a constraint for the needed quantity of Softa stone is written as:

$$80X_1 + 40X_2 \geq 400 \text{ tons (of Softa stone)}$$

Similarly, the constraints for the other stones can be written:

$$60X_1 + 80X_2 \geq 500 \text{ tons (of Harda stone)}$$

$$20X_1 + 60X_2 \geq 180 \text{ tons (of Common stone)}$$

The crew must continue to quarry until at least the minimum requirements for each type of stone are obtained. Since the stones are obtained from the aggregates in fixed proportions, usually there will be an excess of some types. This accounts for the greater-than-or-equal-to ($\geq$) signs in the constraints.

Summarizing, Rollin Along's problem is to choose values of X_1 and X_2 that minimize Z and satisfy the three quantity constraints. That is:

minimize: $\qquad\qquad\qquad Z = X_1 + X_2$

so that: $\qquad\qquad\qquad 80X_1 + 40X_2 \geq 400$

$\qquad\qquad\qquad\qquad\quad 60X_1 + 80X_2 \geq 500$

$\qquad\qquad\qquad\qquad\quad 20X_1 + 60X_2 \geq 180$

and $\qquad\qquad\quad X_1 \geq 0 \quad$ and $\quad X_2 \geq 0$

---

*Subscripts are used throughout the book as a convenience. Readers for whom such notation is a distant recollection should have little difficulty if they remember that subscripts do not imply any algebraic operations. They only distinguish between items. In this instance, the subscripts distinguish the quantities at one quarry from those at the other.

The last condition, that X_1 and X_2 not have negative values, expresses the fact that it isn't possible to work a negative number of days at either quarry.

An important feature of Rollin Along's problem is that the mathematical expressions for the objective equation and the constraints are *linear*. That is, there are no exponents or multiplications of variables. Mathematical problems with a linear objective equation and linear constraints are called *linear programming* or, more accurately, *linear optimization* problems. As already noted, linear programming problems have many important industrial uses and they form the underlying mathematical computer-based technology for the applications in this book.

Since there are only two variables, X_1 and X_2, Rollin Along's linear programming problem can be solved graphically. Figure 1.1(a) illustrates a coordinate system for X_1 and X_2. The areas corresponding to negative values have been shaded to indicate that they are excluded from consideration.

Consider the first constraint, $80X_1 + 40X_2 \geq 400$, which the values of X_1 and X_2 must satisfy. A plot of the constraint line $80X_1 + 40X_2 = 400$ appears in Figure 1.1(b). Allowable values of X_1 and X_2, corresponding to the "greater than" situation, lie on the right-hand side of the constraint line. A little reflection shows that points to the left of the constraint line are inconsistent with the "greater than" requirement of the constraint. Therefore, the triangular area to the left of the constraint line has been shaded to indicate that it is excluded from further consideration.

Similarly, the two other constraint lines (for Harda stone and Common stone) are plotted and the unacceptable areas shaded, as shown in Figure 1.1(c). This completes the graphing of constraint lines.

Now Rollin Along's task is to find an *optimal solution* or solutions, that is, the best pair or pairs of values of X_1 and X_2 that do not violate the constraints. Such values of X_1 and X_2 lie within (or on the boundary of) the acceptable (unshaded) area of Figure 1.1(c).

To begin the search for an optimal solution, arbitrarily suppose that the total quarrying time Z has the value 10 days. Plot the line $Z = X_1 + X_2 = 10$ as in Figure 1.1(d). Every point on the portion of the line $X_1 + X_2 = 10$ within the unshaded area corresponds to a possible way in which the quarries can be worked to obtain the required stone in a total of 10 working days.

However, if the required stone can be obtained in fewer than 10 days, all the better. Try a smaller value, say, $Z = 9$ days. Then the objective equation becomes $Z = X_1 + X_2 = 9$. This line is also plotted in Figure 1.1(d). Again, every point of the line in the unshaded area is a working possibility — but, of course, not necessarily an optimal one.

Note that the two objective lines $\{X_1 + X_2 = 10\}$ and $\{X_1 + X_2 = 9\}$ are parallel and that the latter line lies below and to the left of the former. A straightedge placed along one of them, and moved parallel to itself in the

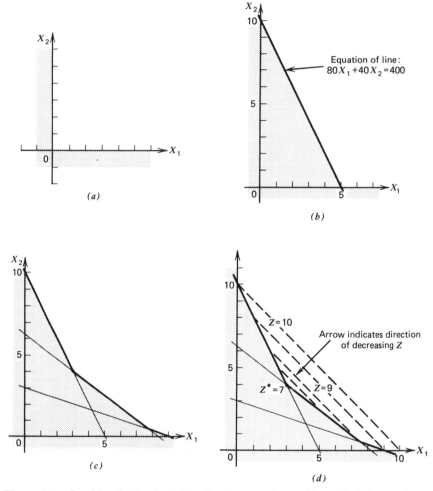

Figure 1.1. Graphic solution for Rollin Along's quarrying problem. Shaded areas denote unacceptable values of X_1 and X_2.

direction of the origin, corresponds to smaller (and, hence, more desirable) values of Z. This parallel movement can continue as long as any point of the acceptable area touches the straightedge. The minimum value of Z is obtained when the parallel movement of the straightedge cannot continue without "losing touch" with the acceptable area. In this example the minimum value of Z (denoted by Z^*) is 7, as shown in Figure 1.1(d). The value $Z^* = 7$ corresponds to the point $X_1 = 3$ and $X_2 = 4$. Rollin Along's problem is solved. Operate the first quarry for 3 days and the second quarry for 4 days. The required quantities of each type of stone will be available in 7 days.

This graphic method of solution, while correct, is of limited practicality. For linear programming problems with more than two variables and/or many constraints, more efficient methods are needed. Fortunately they are readily available as explained in the next chapter.

The graphic method has been used here to help visualize the logic involved in solving linear programming problems. Interested readers can practice obtaining graphic solutions to a few of the linear programs in Problem 10 of Appendix 4. However, this is not necessary to understand the subsequent chapters.

CHAPTER 2

USING LINEAR PROGRAMMING

The quarrying example in the last chapter introduced the mathematical format known as linear programming. Linear programming, or LP, has an important and increasing industrial role. Hundreds of applications, as diverse as setting up automobile production lines, aiding oil refinery management, determining timber production, or preparing hospital menus, have been documented. New uses are still being discovered, and among them are applications to construction management. The discussion here and in subsequent chapters is, of course, limited to the latter.

2.1. GENERAL LINEAR PROGRAMMING FORM

We have already noted that an essential feature of the quarrying example was that both the objective equation and the constraints were linear, that is, no exponents or products of the decision variables appeared in them. In general, all linear programming problems can be expressed in the following form:

minimize (or maximize):

$$Z = c_1X_1 + c_2X_2 + \cdots + c_nX_n \qquad \text{objective equation} \quad (1)$$

such that:
$$a_{11}X_1 + a_{12}X_2 + \cdots + a_{1n}X_n \leq b_1$$

$$\vdots$$

$$a_{k1}X_1 + a_{k2}X_2 + \cdots + a_{kn}X_n \geq b_k \qquad \Bigg\} \quad \text{constraints} \quad (2)$$

$$\vdots$$

$$a_{m1}X_1 + a_{m2}X_2 + \cdots + a_{mn}X_n = b_m$$

and $X_1 \geq 0, X_2 \geq 0, \cdots, X_n \geq 0$ \qquad nonnegativity condition \quad (3) where the quantities $a_{11}, a_{12}, \cdots, a_{mn}, b_1, \cdots, b_k, \cdots, b_m,$ and $c_1, c_2, \cdots, c_n$ are constants. Note that the constraints [Eq. (2)] can be of the "less than," "greater than," or "equality" types. The problem is to select values of the decision variables $X_1, X_2, \cdots, X_n$ that minimize (or maximize, as appropriate) the objective equation [Eq. (1)] and satisfy the constraints [Eq. (2)] and the nonnegativity condition [Eq. (3)].

While the objective equation will usually represent a total cost that is to be minimized or a total profit to be maximized, that is not always the case. For example, in the last chapter the objective was to minimize the total quarrying time $Z = X_1 + X_2$. Comparing this example with Eq. (1), $n = 2$ and the constants c_1 and c_2 are both equal to unity.

Each of these three distinct types of constraints arise in applications:

1. Less-than constraints are usually used to indicate an upper limit on the availability of resources, such as work force, machinery, materials, or money.

2. Greater-than constraints, on the other hand, indicate lower limits on resource utilization or production. In the quarrying example, greater-than constraints expressed required minimum levels of stone.

3. Equal-to constraints, or equality constraints as they are called, occur less frequently. In construction, equality constraints arise to express the requirement that the sum of the parts must equal the whole. For example, the sum of the item bids in a unit price proposal must equal the total bid as explained in Chapter 7.

The nonnegativity condition [Eq. (3)] requires that decision variables not assume values that are negative. Situations can arise when negative values of decision variables are meaningful. For example, to determine a highway profile, decision variables could be used to represent the slopes of successive sections of roadway. Then negative values of decision variables would indicate a decrease in grade and positive values an increase. Fortunately, the nonnegativity condition is not as restrictive as it appears. A variable, say X_k, that can meaningfully have both negative and positive values can always be represented as the difference of two nonnegative variables, that is, $X_k = U_k - V_k$. One simply replaces X_k by $U_k - V_k$ in Eqs. (1) and (2), and includes $U_k \geq 0$ and $V_k \geq 0$ in Eq. (3). Therefore, the general linear programming form of Eqs. (1)–(3) remains intact.

Every managerial problem has an objective and every practical problem has constraints. Often these problems can be expressed in the general linear programming form [Eqs. (1)–(3)] which nearly always has simple, efficient, and relatively inexpensive techniques available for its solution. The next section describes these possibilities.

2.2. OBTAINING SOLUTIONS

Earlier the practical limitations of obtaining solutions graphically were noted. Linear programming problems can also be solved by "hand," utilizing a solution procedure known as the *simplex method*. Many books discuss the method in detail, but for convenience a simplified step-by-step procedure is explained in Appendix 2. While only "grocery store" arithmetic is needed to obtain solutions using the simplex method, its manual application is limited to smaller problems, usually with less than a dozen variables and/or constraints. The required arithmetic becomes taxing for the larger problems that arise in practical applications. Fortunately, attractive computer-based procedures, based on the simplex method, are available so that there is virtually no practical limit to problem size.

Display 2.1 is one example of computer input and output. It shows both the formulation and the computer-aided solution to the quarrying prob-

```
#
RUN $DELIBR/LP
#RUNNING 0417
TYPE HELP IF YOU NEED IT
-->   #?
LOAD
ENTER OBJECTIVE FUNCTION:
OBJ*FN :      MIN    1X[1] + 1X[2]
ENTER CONSTRAINTS:
CON1 :              80X[1] + 40X[2] >= 400
CON2 :              60X[1] + 80X[2] >= 500
CON3 :              20X[1] + 60X[2] >= 180
CON4 :
-->  SOLVE

                  X[1]      X[2]       RHS
          ********************************
OBJ*FN *   1.00      1.00       0.00  *
CON1   * -80.00    -40.00    -400.00  *
CON2   * -60.00    -80.00    -500.00  *
CON3   * -20.00    -60.00    -180.00  *
          ********************************  •
          TABLEAU 0

                  CON1      CON2       RHS
          *******************************
OBJ*FN *   0.01      0.01      -7.00  *
X[1]   *  -0.02      0.01       3.00  *
X[2]   *   0.02     -0.02       4.00  *
CON3   *   0.50     -1.00     120.00  *
          *******************************
          TABLEAU 2

OBJECTIVE FUNCTION ATTAINS A MINIMUM VALUE OF 7 AT:
               X[1] =        3.00
               X[2] =        4.00

-->  STOP
```

Display 2.1. Computer input and output.

lem which was solved graphically in Chapter 1. The shaded type indicates input, that is, information entered from a keyboard. The other portions are the output or product of the computer. Specifically:

RUN $DELIBR/LP:	Prepares our computer for solving a linear program. The computer types a prompt (-->), indicating that it requires a command.
LOAD:	Initiates the sequence for loading the problem. The computer responds by requesting the objective function.
MIN 1X[1] + 1X[2]:	Indicates the objective function. The computer responds by requesting the first constraint, that is, CON 1.
80X[1] + 40X[2] >= 400:	Enters the first constraint. The computer responds with CON 2, and so on. When all constraints have been entered, the computer types a second prompt (-->) for the next command.
SOLVE:	Initiates solution of the input problem.

The computer then outputs a series of tableaus (indicating its progress toward the solution) and, finally, the optimal values of the objective equation $\{=7\}$ and each decision variable $\{X_1 = 3, X_2 = 4\}$. Subsequently, the computer types a prompt for the next command or problem. Entering STOP indeed stops the program. The solution of the quarrying problem (Display 2.1) was obtained in less than 5 minutes for 17¢, using a Burroughs B7700 computer.

Readers should spend a few additional minutes gaining familiarity with the format of Display 2.1. For convenience, the same computer and software program are used in examples throughout the text. Of course, readers can enter the same data to a more familiar program and/or computer and simply substitute their outputs for the displays throughout the book.

The means to obtain computer-aided solutions to linear programming problems have developed rapidly during the past two decades. Linear programming problems can now be solved on small as well as on large computers, including the now widely available and reasonably priced portable (or personal) computers (see Appendix 3). For practical purposes it is not necessary to understand how the computer obtained the solutions, and no particular knowledge of computers or mathematics is needed to use these computer-aided solution techniques effectively. The construction manager needs only to formulate the problem (in much the way we formulated the quarrying problem of Chapter 1), respond to the computer's requests for input, and develop skill in interpreting and acting upon the results.

Companies having access to a computer, including hand-held ones, can consult the user manuals and their references for assistance. Others may seek professional sources of assistance, for example, under "Data Processing Service" in the Yellow Pages. Universities and colleges also have computing capabilities that include solving linear programming problems. While regulations vary, one usually can purchase computer time and employ students part-time to assist in obtaining solutions.

A construction manager should be able to "get the hang" of obtaining computer-aided linear programming solutions as conveniently as other regularly used services. The main impediment for many seems to be the psychological inertia of beginning something new. Once this inertia is overcome, a truly impressive computational technology can be utilized.

2.3. MANAGING COMPUTER OUTPUT

Suppose that a decision-making situation can be described reasonably by a linear programming problem, that the numerical data have been assembled, and that an optimal solution has been obtained. This solution may be all that is required for an operating decision. Sometimes, however, further analyses are desirable, particularly when some of the numerical data are uncertain or subject to change, or perhaps when the problem formulation was incomplete or unnecessarily restrictive. The importance and versatility of linear programming stems from its ability to cope with such circumstances. The discussion that follows suggests some of its principal features.

i) *Solution Sensitivity.* Numerical data are subject to alteration for a variety of reasons. Sometimes there is uncertainty in the measurement or estimation of quantities. Possibly, working or market conditions have changed. For example, suppose that the required quantity of Softa stone in the quarrying problem is increased from 400 to 500 tons. It is important to know how such changes affect the solution. One way to find out whether the quarrying time is sensitive to the change in Softa stone is simply to replace 400 by 500 in the first constraint and run the computer program again. However, even this may not be necessary since most computer programs routinely provide sensitivity information when they output solutions. The study of solution changes for changes in numerical data is called a *sensitivity analysis* or *ranging analysis.*

For the quarrying problem, had the word SENSITIVITY been entered as input after the constraints had been entered, the result would be Display 2.2 instead of Display 2.1. (Note: the word NONE entered as input after the constraints deletes the tableaus from the computer output.)

```
#
RUN #DELIBR/LP
#RUNNING 0445
TYPE HELP IF YOU NEED IT
-->  #?
LOAD
ENTER OBJECTIVE FUNCTION:
OBJ*FN:   MIN X[1] + X[2]
ENTER CONSTRAINTS:
CON1:   80X[1] + 40X[2] >= 400
CON2:   60X[1] + 80X[2] >= 500
CON3:   20X[1] + 60X[2] >= 180
CON4:
-->  NONE
-->  SENSITIVITY
-->  SOLVE

OBJECTIVE FUNCTION ATTAINS A MINIMUM VALUE OF 7 AT:
             X[1] =        3.00
             X[2] =        4.00

SENSITIVITY ANALYSIS:

   WITHIN THE RANGE 250 TO 640, EACH UNIT OF CON1 ADDS 0.005 TO THE
COST.  CURRENTLY THE CON1 CONSTRAINT IS SET AT 400.

   WITHIN THE RANGE 380 TO 800, EACH UNIT OF CON2 ADDS 0.01 TO THE
COST.  CURRENTLY THE CON2 CONSTRAINT IS SET AT 500.

   THE CON3 CONSTRAINT IS MET WITH 120 UNITS TO SPARE.  CURRENTLY THIS
IS SET AT 180.

-->  STOP
```

Display 2.2. Computer input/output with sensitivity analysis.

The sensitivity analysis included in Display 2.2 indicates that a unit change in the required quantity of Softa stone (CON 1) within the range of 250 to 640 tons adds 0.005 (day) to the minimum cost (total time). Therefore a 100-unit (ton) increase in the Softa stone (from 400 to 500) increases the minimum quarrying time by one-half day (0.005×100) to 7.5 days. Problem 2 in Appendix 4 asks the reader to verify this.

The sensitivity analysis also indicates that 120 tons of Common stone (CON 3) are available beyond the required amount. Therefore, no additional computation is needed to conclude that the requirement for Common stone could be increased from 180 to 300 tons without otherwise changing the indicated solution.

The main point of this discussion is that a sensitivity analysis is readily available to assist in understanding how changes or errors in the numerical data affect the solution at hand. Incidentally, the cost of the solution and the sensitivity analysis in Display 2.2 was 34¢ on the Burroughs B7700 computer.

ii) *Adding or Removing Constraints.* Sometimes it is useful to explore the effect upon the solution of adding or removing some constraints. For example, it may be possible to hire or lease additional units of a constrained resource. Comparison of the linear programming solutions with and without the corresponding constraint provides insight into the advantage (or disadvantage) of obtaining additional resources. Similarly, one could add or remove a constraint to ascertain how the profitability changes if certain demands are lax (see Problem 2 in Appendix 4). To compare solutions, simply modify the constraints and solve the revised linear programming problem. In a sense, this is a form of solution sensitivity.

iii) *Multiple Solutions.* The solution to a linear programming problem, that is, the optimal values of the objective equation and the decision variables, is the best, or optimum, achievable (while satisfying the constraints). However, there may be other values of the decision variables which also satisfy the constraints and yield the same optimal value for the objective equation, that is, there may be *multiple optimal solutions* (or *multiple solutions,* for short).

In the quarrying problem of Chapter 1, assume for illustrative purposes that the daily output of Harda stone from Quarry 2 is reduced by 20 tons per day, and that the required quantity of Harda stone is reduced by 80 tons. That is, the revised constraint for Harda stone is

$$60X_1 + 60X_2 \geq 420 \text{ tons (of Harda stone)}$$

Figure 2.1 illustrates the graphic method for this situation. Note that as the objective line is moved toward the origin, it finally coincides with a boundary of the acceptable area. This means that any points on the segment between the vertices marked A and B have the same optimal value $Z^* = 7$. The values $X_1 = 3$ and $X_2 = 4$, corresponding to the

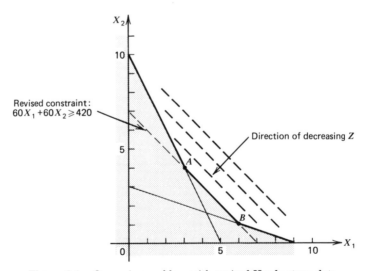

Figure 2.1. Quarrying problem with revised Harda stone data.

vertex A, are still an optimal solution. However, other values of X_1 and X_2, corresponding to points along the segment, also yield the same minimum value for the objective. They are multiple solutions.

Multiple solutions occur in many practical linear programming problems. Fortunately, linear programming computer programs clearly indicate when multiple solutions are present. While these programs can also provide the multiple solutions, obtaining all of them can be vexing since there is no certain rule to indicate their numbers.

At first sight multiple solutions appear to be an annoying complication. Actually, they have a practical advantage. Mathematical descriptions, such as Eqs. (1)–(3), rarely are accurate representations of real problems. Relevant factors are always excluded from a mathematical description for one reason or another. Company prestige, project aesthetics, and morale are just a few examples of relevant considerations that are difficult to describe mathematically. The multiple solutions permit a manager to choose preferentially among mathematically equivalent solutions.

iv) *Integer-Valued Solutions.* Sometimes only whole numbers, or integer values of the decision variables, are sensible. For example, fractions of trucks or people may be meaningless in some problem contexts. It is tempting to simply round off or truncate noninteger values of the ordinary linear programming solution. However, caution is advised; the results may be incorrect.

To illustrate, consider the following linear programming problem:

maximize: $\qquad\qquad Z = 7X_1 + 10X_2$

such that: $\qquad\qquad\qquad\quad X_1 \leq 3$

$$2X_1 + 5X_2 \leq 15$$

and $\qquad\qquad\qquad X_1 \geq 0, \qquad X_2 \geq 0$

The solution, shown graphically in Figure 2.2, is $X_1 = 3$, $X_2 = 1.8$, and $Z^* = 39$. If an integer-valued solution is required, one might suggest rounding X_2 upward to 2. However, this would violate the second constraint, since $2(3) + 5(2) = 16$. If one truncates so that $X_2 = 1$, the constraints are satisfied and the value of Z is $7(3) + 10(1) = 31$. However, this is less than the correct integer-valued solution of $X_1 = X_2 = 2$ and $Z^* = 34$.

Computer programs are available to solve linear programming problems requiring integer-valued solutions. However, computational costs are greater than for the ordinary linear programming solutions we have been discussing. Some rules of thumb exist for approximating the cost of integer-valued solutions, but they are not always reliable. A manager having frequent need for integer-valued solutions should seek assistance beyond the scope of the text. Some simple advice is to obtain an estimate of the computational cost beforehand and monitor it during computation.

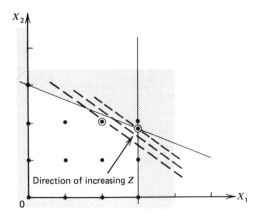

Figure 2.2. Graphic solution to problem with integer considerations.

v) *Problem Size and Computation Costs.* People who speak of the size of linear programming problems usually mean some indication of the number of variables and/or the number of constraints. For most practical purposes there is no limitation on the size of the linear programming problem that can be solved. It is a common industrial practice to solve linear programming problems with variables and constraints numbering in the thousands.

Increasing problem size, of course, tends to increase computational costs; but not always. There is no precise relationship between problem size and computational cost. The size and type of computer that is used, the particular program used by the computer, and the extent to which the numerical data contain many "easy numbers" are factors that influence the computational time and, hence, the cost. As a guide, additional constraints tend to increase computational costs more rapidly than additional variables. It is fair to say that if your decision-making situation can reasonably be represented by a linear programming problem, the computational costs will probably be minor when compared with the savings from an improved decision.

2.4. FORMULATION EXAMPLES

To assist the reader to develop skills of formulating linear programming problems, extensions of the quarrying problem appear in the following two examples.

Example 1. Quarrying at Least Cost

In the original quarrying example of Chapter 1, Rollin Along was interested in quarrying the required quantities of stone in the shortest time. Instead, suppose that the objective is to minimize quarrying costs.

If the daily costs of operation in Quarry 1 and Quarry 2 are the same, say $500 per day, the objective equation becomes $Z = 500X_1 + 500X_2$. The constraints remain unchanged. Solving this new linear programming problem yields $Z^* = 3500$, the minimum total cost, and $X_1 = 3$, $X_2 = 4$ (see Figure 2.3). Interestingly, the values for the decision variables have not changed from those for the original problem. The reason is clear when the graphic solution is examined. The objective line $Z = 500X_1 + 500X_2$ is parallel to the line $Z = X_1 + X_2$. Since both objective equations are minimized by moving objective lines toward the origin, the optimal solution point (a vertex of the acceptable area) is the same as before.

Now suppose that the total quarrying costs are not the same. For example, say $c_1 = \$400$ and $c_2 = \$1400$ per day of operation at Quarry 1 and Quarry 2, respectively. The objective equation is $Z = 400X_1 + 1400X_2$, and the solution appears in Display 2.3. As expected, the cost advantage of Quarry 1 is apparent. Here the minimum objective value is $Z^* = \$3600$ when $X_1 = 9$ and $X_2 = 0$.

Rollin Along now knows that the time to obtain the required stone at minimum cost ($3600) is 9 days. But this is 2 days more than the original shortest time solution. If Rollin Along cannot quarry longer than 8 days, the constraint

$$X_1 + X_2 \le 8$$

is included in the problem. The new solution is $Z^* = \$4200$ and $X_1 = 7$ and $X_2 = 1$, as shown in Display 2.4. Management can decide whether it is worth an additional $600 (= $4200 − $3600) to obtain the required stone a day earlier. Can you show that the additional cost of reducing the quarrying time by another day is $2600? (See Problem 2 in Appendix 4.)

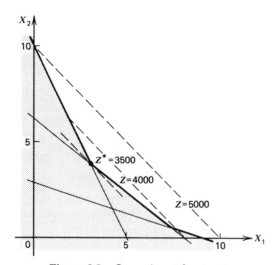

Figure 2.3. Quarrying at least cost.

```
#
RUN $DELIBR/LP
#RUNNING 0457
TYPE HELP IF YOU NEED IT
-->   #?
LOAD
ENTER OBJECTIVE FUNCTION:
OBJ*FN: MIN   400X[1] + 1400X[2]
ENTER CONSTRAINTS:
CON1:           80X[1] +    40X[2] >= 400
CON2:           60X[1] +    80X[2] >= 500
CON3:           20X[1] +    60X[2] >= 180
CON4:
-->   SOLVE

              X[1]        X[2]        RHS
        ********************************
OBJ*FN *    400.00     1400.00       0.00  *
CON1   *    -80.00      -40.00    -400.00  *
CON2   *    -60.00      -80.00    -500.00  *
CON3   *    -20.00      -60.00    -180.00  *
        ********************************
              TABLEAU 0

              CON3        X[2]        RHS
        ***********************************
OBJ*FN *     20.00      200.00    -3600.00  *
CON1   *     -4.00      200.00      320.00  *
X[1]   *     -0.05        3.00        9.00  *
CON2   *     -3.00      100.00       40.00  *
        ***********************************
              TABLEAU 2

OBJECTIVE FUNCTION ATTAINS A MINIMUM VALUE OF 3600 AT:
              X[1]              9.00

      THE OTHER VARIABLE HAS A VALUE OF ZERO.

-->   STOP
```

Display 2.3. Quarrying with unequal unit costs.

Rollin Along can evaluate the trade-off between minimum cost and minimum time in still another way. Suppose management estimates that each day of delay in obtaining the required quantities of stone costs the firm $1000. The delay cost is then $1000 × $(X_1 + X_2)$. The two costs (quarrying and delay) can easily be combined into a single total-cost objective equation as:

$$\text{minimize:}\quad Z = 400X_1 + 1400X_2 + 1000(X_1 + X_2)$$
$$= 1400X_1 + 2400X_2$$

Using only the three quantity-of-stone constraints of Chapter 1, when $X_1 = 7.8$ and $X_2 = 0.4$, the minimum value of Z is $11,880 (see Display 2.5). If integer values of the decision variables are desired, one types INTEGER after the prompt (-->) that follows the noninteger solution and SOLVEs the linear program again. The optimal integer values are $X_1 = 7.0$ and $X_2 = 1.0$, and the minimum cost is $Z^* = $12,200.

```
#
RUN $DELIBR/LP
#RUNNING 0465
TYPE HELP IF YOU NEED IT
-->  #?
LOAD
ENTER OBJECTIVE FUNCTION:
OBJ*FN: MIN   400X[1] + 1400X[2]
ENTER CONSTRAINTS:
CON1:          80X[1] +    40X[2] >= 400
CON2:          60X[1] +    80X[2] >= 500
CON3:          20X[1] +    60X[2] >= 180
CON4:           1X[1] +     1X[2] <=   8
CON5:
-->  SOLVE

               X[1]        X[2]        RHS
          ******************************
OBJ*FN *  400.00     1400.00        0.00  *
CON1   *  -80.00      -40.00     -400.00  *
CON2   *  -60.00      -80.00     -500.00  *
CON3   *  -20.00      -60.00     -180.00  *
CON4   *    1.00        1.00        8.00  *
          ******************************
          TABLEAU 0

               CON2        CON4        RHS
          ********************************
OBJ*FN *   50.00      2600.00    -4200.00  *
CON1   *    2.00       200.00      200.00  *
X[1]   *    0.05         4.00        7.00  *
CON3   *   -2.00      -100.00       20.00  *
X[2]   *   -0.05        -3.00        1.00  *
          ********************************
          TABLEAU 4

OBJECTIVE FUNCTION ATTAINS A MINIMUM VALUE OF 4200 AT:
                   X[1] =         7.00
                   X[2] =         1.00

-->  STOP
```

Display 2.4. Quarrying at least cost with a time constraint.

Finally, suppose that Rollin Along can obtain Common stone from a commercial source for $14 per ton. How should this source of supply affect the decision? To find out, first define the decision variable Y_C as the quantity (in tons) of Common stone to be purchased commercially (assume that there are no delivery delays). The total-cost objective equation can then be written:

minimize: $Z = 400X_1 + 1400X_2 + 1000(X_1 + X_2) + 14Y_C$

$= 1400X_1 + 2400X_2 + 14Y_C$

The constraints specifying the minimum quantity of Softa stone and Harda stone are not affected, but since Common stone is now available from three sources, its constraint becomes:

$$20X_1 + 60X_2 + Y_C \geq 180$$

```
#
RUN $DELIBR/LP
#RUNNING 0485
TYPE HELP IF YOU NEED IT
-->  #?
LOAD
ENTER OBJECTIVE FUNCTION:
OBJ*FN: MIN  1400X[1] + 2400X[2]
ENTER CONSTRAINTS:
CON1:          80X[1[ +    40X[2] >= 400
CON2:          60X[1] +    80X[2] >= 500
CON3:          20X[1] +    60X[2] >= 180
CON4:
-->  SOLVE

             X[1]       X[2]       RHS
        ********************************
OBJ*FN * 1400.00    2400.00      0.00  *
CON1   *  -80.00     -40.00   -400.00  *
CON2   *  -60.00     -80.00   -500.00  *
CON3   *  -20.00     -60.00   -180.00  *
        ********************************
             TABLEAU 0

             CON2       CON3       RHS
        ************************************
OBJ*FN *    18.00      16.00  -11880.00  *
CON1   *    -2.00       2.00     240.00  *
X[1]   *    -0.03       0.04       7.80  *
X[2]   *     0.01      -0.03       0.40  *
        ************************************
             TABLEAU 2

OBJECTIVE FUNCTION ATTAINS A MINIMUM VALUE OF 11880 AT:
                   X[1] =          7.80
                   X[2] =          0.40

-->  INTEGER
-->  NONE
-->  SOLVE

OBJECTIVE FUNCTION ATTAINS A MINIMUM VALUE OF 12200 AT:
                   X[1] =          7.00
                   X[2] =          1.00

-->  STOP
```

Display 2.5. Quarrying with a cost–time trade-off.

The computer-aided solution in Display 2.6 shows that $Z^* = \$11,853.33$, $X_1 = 8.33$, $X_2 = 0$, and $Y_C = 13.33$. If an integer solution is sought, Display 2.6 shows that $Z^* = \$12,200$ when $X_1 = 7$, $X_2 = 1$, and $Y_C = 0$. This is a less costly solution than an improper rounding of X_1 to 9 and Y_C to zero (for which $Z^* = \$12,600$).

Example 2. Quarrying over Periods of Time

The use of linear programming to here has been for "one-shot" decisions. It can also be used for a sequence of decisions over a period of time.

    Suppose that Rollin Along's construction operations are to begin in a

```
#
RUN $DELIBR/LP
#RUNNING 0498
TYPE HELP IF YOU NEED IT
--> #?
LOAD
ENTER OBJECTIVE FUNCTION:
OBJ*FN: MIN   1400X[1] + 2400X[2] +  14Y[C]
ENTER CONSTRAINTS:
CON1:         80X[1] +  40X[2]          >= 400
CON2:         60X[1] +  80X[2]          >= 500
CON3:         20X[1] +  60X[2] +  1Y[C] >= 180
CON4:
--> SOLVE

              X[1]      X[2]      Y[C]      RHS
        *******************************************
OBJ*FN * 1400.00   2400.00     14.00      0.00  *
CON1   *  -80.00    -40.00      0.00   -400.00  *
CON2   *  -60.00    -80.00      0.00   -500.00  *
CON3   *  -20.00    -60.00     -1.00   -180.00  *
        *******************************************
        TABLEAU 0

              CON2      X[2]      CON3      RHS
        ***********************************************
OBJ*FN *    18.67     66.67     14.00  -11853.33  *
CON1   *    -1.33     66.67      0.00    266.67  *
X[1]   *    -0.02      1.33      0.00      8.33  *
Y[B]   *     0.33     33.33     -1.00     13.33  *
        ***********************************************
        TABLEAU 2

OBJECTIVE FUNCTION ATTAINS A MINIMUM VALUE OF 11853.333 AT:
              X[1]          8.33
              Y[C]         13.33

      THE OTHER VARIABLE HAS A VALUE OF ZERO.

--> INTEGER
--> NONE
--> SOLVE

OBJECTIVE FUNCTION ATTAINS A MINIMUM VALUE OF 12200 AT:
              X[1] =        7.00
              X[2] =        1.00

      THE OTHER VARIABLE HAS A VALUE OF ZERO.

--> STOP
```

Display 2.6. Quarrying when a commercial source is available.

week, and a three-week forecast for quantities (in tons per week) of needed stone is:

Stone	Construction Week		
	1	2	3
Softa	400	600	660
Harda	500	600	600
Common	180	320	340

Again, assume that Rollin Along has a single crew available for up to 5 days per week at the two quarries. The respective daily operating costs at the two quarries are \$400 and \$1400; and the daily yields are 80, 60, and 20 tons and 40, 80, and 60 tons of the respective types of stone.

In addition, the commercial source of stone, identified in the previous example, has expanded its production operations and can provide stone of any type at a flat rate of \$12 per ton. This source has an ample supply of Softa stone, but its current supplies of Harda and Common stones are limited to 600 and 200 tons, respectively. However, effectively unlimited supplies of Harda and Common stones are expected in time for the third week of construction (but not earlier).

Site storage of stone poses no problem for Rollin Along. However, the needed weekly quantities must be on hand at the beginning of each week to avoid interference with site operations.

Rollin Along must decide where to assign the quarry crew and how much stone to purchase in order to obtain the needed stones at least cost.

Earlier in this chapter the symbols X_1 and X_2 were used to denote the number of days the quarry crew was to work the first and second quarries, respectively. Here the situation is a bit more complex since the number of days to work each quarry may vary from week to week as requirements change. To take the timing into account, use double subscripts. That is, X_{11}, X_{12}, and X_{13} can represent the number of days to work the first quarry during the week preceding the first, second, and third weeks of construction, respectively. Similarly, for the second quarry use X_{21}, X_{22}, and X_{23}. Note that the first subscript identifies the quarry, and the second the week of construction.

Variables are also needed to represent the quantities of stone that can be purchased. Again, double subscripted variables are convenient. Use Y_{S1}, Y_{S2}, and Y_{S3} for quantities of Softa stone to be purchased immediately preceding the first, second, and third weeks of construction, respectively; Y_{H1}, Y_{H2}, and Y_{H3} for the Harda stone; and Y_{C1}, Y_{C2}, and Y_{C3} for the Common stone.

Now Rollin Along's problem of minimizing the total cost of stone can be formulated beginning with the objective equation as follows:

minimize:

$$Z = 400X_{11} + 400X_{12} + 400X_{13} + 1400X_{21} + 1400X_{22} + 1400X_{23}$$
$$+ 12Y_{S1} + 12Y_{S2} + 12Y_{S3} + 12Y_{H1} + 12Y_{H2} + 12Y_{H3}$$
$$+ 12Y_{C1} + 12Y_{C2} + 12Y_{C3}$$

The first three terms represent the costs at the first quarry, the next three terms those at the second quarry, and the remaining terms express the cost of purchased stone, if any.

For the constraints, at least 400 tons of Softa stone is needed for work in the first week, that is:

$$80X_{11} + 40X_{21} + Y_{S1} \geq 400 \text{ tons}$$

Clearly, any excess stone that is not used during the first week will be available to meet the requirements in the second week, and so on. For Softa stone requirements in the second week, write:

$$(80X_{11} + 40X_{21} + Y_{S1} - 400) + 80X_{12} + 40X_{22} + Y_{S2} \geq 600 \text{ tons}$$

The quantity $(80X_{11} + 40X_{21} + Y_{S1} - 400)$ is the excess, if any, of Softa stone not used in the first week. This last expression can be rewritten as:

$$80X_{11} + 80X_{12} + 40X_{21} + 40X_{22} + Y_{S1} + Y_{S2} \geq 1000 \text{ tons}$$

Similarly, for the third week:

$$80X_{11} + 80X_{12} + 80X_{13} + 40X_{21} + 40X_{22}$$
$$+ 40X_{23} + Y_{S1} + Y_{S2} + Y_{S3} \geq 1660 \text{ tons}$$

In the same way, constraints are written for Harda and Common stones. Therefore, there are nine constraints (one for each type of stone for each of three weeks) to ensure the needed quantities. These appear in Display 2.7.

To limit the work week to five days, these additional constraints are necessary:

$$X_{11} + X_{21} \leq 5 \text{ days}$$
$$X_{12} + X_{22} \leq 5 \text{ days}$$
$$X_{13} + X_{23} \leq 5 \text{ days}$$

Finally, constraints are needed because of the limited availability of Harda and Common stones (recall that the external supply of Softa stone is unlimited). These are written as:

$$Y_{H1} + Y_{H2} \leq 600 \text{ tons}$$
$$Y_{C1} + Y_{C2} \leq 200 \text{ tons}$$

Note that these constraints only involve variables for the first and second weeks. The reason, of course, is that the supply available for the third week (Y_{H3} and Y_{C3}) is effectively unlimited.

Summarizing, Rollin Along's problem has been formulated as a linear programming problem. The objective is to minimize total cost such that 14 linear constraints (nine quantity constraints, three work week constraints, and the two external supply constraints) are satisfied. Of course, none of the variables can be permitted to have negative values. The formulation appears in Display 2.7 along with an optimal solution with $Z^* = \$29,500$.

Note that Display 2.7 is somewhat different than earlier ones. The reason is that the larger size of this problem required use of a somewhat more powerful computer program for its solution. The procedure for

FORMULATION:

```
MINIMIZE OBJ*FN = 400 X11 +400 X12 +400 X13 +1400 X21 +1400 X22
        +1400 X23 +12 YS1 +12 YS2 +12 YS3 +12 YH1 +12 YH2
        +12 YH3 +12 YC1 +12 YC2 +12 YC3
CON1: 80 X11 +40 X21 + YS1 >= 400
CON2: 80 X11 +80 X12 +40 X21 +40 X22 + YS1 + YS2 >= 1000
CON3: 80 X11 +80 X12 +80 X13 +40 X21 +40 X22 +40 X23 + YS1
      + YS2 + YS3 >= 1660
CON4: 60 X11 +80 X21 + YH1 >= 500
CON5: 60 X11 +60 X12 +80 X21 +80 X22 + YH1 + YH2 >= 1100
CON6: 60 X11 +60 X12 +60 X13 +80 X21 +80 X22 +80 X23 + YH1
      + YH2 + YH3 >= 1700
CON7: 20 X11 +60 X21 + YC1 >= 180
CON8: 20 X11 +20 X12 +60 X21 +60 X22 + YC1 + YC2 >= 500
CON9: 20 X11 +20 X12 +20 X13 +60 X21 +60 X22 +60 X23 + YC1
      + YC2 + YC3 >= 840
CON10:  X11 + X21 <= 5
CON11:  X12 + X22 <= 5
CON12:  X13 + X23 <= 5
CON13:  YH1 + YH2 <= 600
CON14:  YC1 + YC2 <= 200
```

SOLUTION:

NAME	ACTIVITY	SLACK ACTIVITY
OBJ*FN	29500.00000	-29500.00000
CON1	860.00000	-460.00000
CON2	1260.00000	-260.00000
CON3	1660.00000	.
CON4	950.00000	-450.00000
CON5	1250.00000	-150.00000
CON6	1700.00000	.
CON7	400.00000	-220.00000
CON8	500.00000	.
CON9	840.00000	.
CON10	5.00000	.
CON11	5.00000	.
CON12	5.00000	.
CON13	600.00000	.
CON14	200.00000	.
X11	2.50000	
X12	5.00000	
X13	5.00000	
X21	2.50000	
X22	.	
X23	.	
YS1	560.00000	
YS2	.	
YS3	.	
YH1	600.00000	
YH2	.	
YH3	150.00000	
YC1	200.00000	
YC2	.	
YC3	240.00000	

Display 2.7. Quarrying over time.

loading this problem is much the same as before (recall the discussion for Display 2.1). However, the output format is different. In Display 2.7, the computer output includes not only the values of the decision variables but also the status of each constraint. The column labeled ACTIVITY indicates that 860 tons of Softa stone will be available for the first week of construction, while the SLACK ACTIVITY column indicates that this is 460 tons more than is required. Similarly, for the second week, 260 tons more of Softa stone than required will be available. Since the current solution has $Y_{S1} = 560$ and $Y_{S2} = Y_{S3} = 0$, Rollin Along might consider postponing delivery of some of the Softa stone until the second and third weeks. Similar remarks can be made for the Harda and Common stones purchased during the first week. The computational cost to obtain the results of Display 2.7 was 55¢.

CHAPTER 3

BLENDING AGGREGATES

Material blends needed to meet quantity and contract specifications are obtained by blending aggregate supplies of given amounts and characteristics. The problem is to blend aggregates competently and economically. An example clarifies ideas.

3.1. MIXAN BLENDS UNLTD.

Mixan Blends Unltd. must prepare 100 tons of asphalt mix for a mall parking lot. The hot-mix (aggregate) gradation requirement set forth in the contract specifications is given in Table 3.1

Mixan Blends has three sources of aggregate. Two of them are local suppliers of aggregate and the third supplies a commercial filler. Each material meets quality specifications (hardness, strength, soundness, and cleanliness), but none, individually, meets gradation requirements. The relevant gradation and cost data appear in Table 3.2

TABLE 3.1. Contract Specifications

Sieve Size	Percent Passing
1 inch	100% (by weight)
$\frac{3}{4}$ inch	75–100%
$\frac{3}{8}$ inch	45–70%
No. 4	30–55%
No. 8	20–35%
No. 50	5–15%
No. 200	2–8%
Asphalt cement	5% of total mix weight

TABLE 3.2. Gradation and Cost Data

Aggregate Source	Percent Passing Each Sieve Size (by weight)							Cost ($/ton)	
	1 inch	¾ inch	⅜ inch	No. 4	No. 8	No. 50	No. 200	Purchase Price	Blending (and Handling)
Supplier I	100	95	60	40	10	0	0	17	10
Supplier II	100	100	100	85	70	20	3	19	10
Filler	100	100	100	100	100	96	74	25	10

3.2. FORMULATING MIXAN BLENDS' PROBLEM

A linear optimization can help Mixan Blends select an economic mix. Let X_1, X_2, and X_3 represent the number of tons of each aggregate in the final mix. The objective, to minimize the total cost of purchase and blending, is expressed by the objective equation:

minimize:

$$Z = 27X_1 + 29X_2 + 35X_3$$

The coefficients of the decision variables are the cost per ton of purchasing and blending the aggregate from each supplier. For example, the coefficient of X_1 is obtained from the data in Table 3.2 as \$27 (= 17 + 10); and so on.

Appropriate constraints are needed to ensure that the final blend satisfies the gradation requirements. Since each of the three aggregates meets the gradation requirements for 1-inch and ¾-inch sieves, any combination of them will also be satisfactory. The first aggregate satisfies the ⅜-inch sieve requirement (at 60%), but the second and third aggregates do not. To ensure that the final mix meets the ⅜-inch sieve requirement, write the proportion:

$$0.45 \leq \frac{0.60X_1 + 1.00X_2 + 1.00X_3}{X_1 + X_2 + X_3} \leq 0.70$$

The numerator is the tonnage of final blend passed by the ⅜-inch sieve, that is, 60% of X_1 plus 100% of X_2 and X_3. The denominator is the total tonnage. Actually, the above expression can be written as two constraints:

$$\frac{0.60X_1 + 1.00X_2 + 1.00X_3}{X_1 + X_2 + X_3} \geq 0.45$$

and

$$\frac{0.60X_1 + 1.00X_2 + 1.00X_3}{X_1 + X_2 + X_3} \leq 0.70$$

which simplify to:

$$0.15X_1 + 0.55X_2 + 0.55X_3 \geq 0$$
$$-0.10X_1 + 0.30X_2 + 0.30X_3 \leq 0$$
$\frac{3}{8}$-inch sieve

Similarly, constraints for the remaining gradations can be expressed as:

$$0.10X_1 + 0.55X_2 + 0.70X_3 \geq 0$$
$$-0.15X_1 + 0.30X_2 + 0.45X_3 \leq 0$$
No. 4 sieve

$$-0.10X_1 + 0.50X_2 + 0.80X_3 \geq 0$$
$$-0.25X_1 + 0.35X_2 + 0.65X_3 \leq 0$$
No. 8 sieve

$$-0.05X_1 + 0.15X_2 + 0.91X_3 \geq 0$$
$$-0.15X_1 + 0.05X_2 + 0.81X_3 \leq 0$$
No. 50 sieve

$$-0.02X_1 + 0.01X_2 + 0.72X_3 \geq 0$$
$$-0.08X_1 - 0.05X_2 + 0.66X_3 \leq 0$$
No. 200 sieve

Other characteristics of the available aggregates meet contract specifications, so constraints for them are unnecessary.

Since 5% (or 5 tons) of the required 100 tons is to be asphalt cement, the total aggregate blend need only weigh 95 tons. Therefore, include the quantity constraint:

$$X_1 + X_2 + X_3 = 95$$

Of course, if Mixan Blends was interested in more than 95 tons of aggregate, perhaps to stockpile or to take advantage of quantity discounts, this equality sign could be replaced by a greater-than sign. The formulation of Mixan Blends' problem is complete as shown in Display 3.1. The computer-aided solution is:

$$Z^* = \$2608.66$$

$$X_1 = 80.37, \qquad X_2 = 12.33, \qquad X_3 = 2.40$$

In this example, the sources of the aggregates were adequate to meet the requirements. Sometimes this is not the case. Suppose, for example, that the gradation requirement for the No. 4 sieve was 25–45%. This affects the third and fourth constraints above. The computer printout for the revised formulation, Display 3.2, indicates that the problem cannot be solved because the gradation characteristics of the aggregates are not adequate to meet the requirements. Before the job can be completed, Mixan Blends will have to seek additional aggregate sources or request a waiver on some of the gradation requirements.

As the number of available sources of aggregates increases, so does the number of managerial choices from which least-cost solutions can be

```
#
RUN $DELIBR/LP
#RUNNING 8580
TYPE HELP IF YOU NEED IT
-->   #?
LOAD
ENTER OBJECTIVE FUNCTION:
OBJ*FN: MIN    27X1 +    29X2 +    35X3
ENTER CONSTRAINTS:
CON1:         0.15X1 + 0.55X2 + 0.55X3 >= 0
CON2:        -0.10X1 + 0.30X2 + 0.30X3 <= 0
CON3:         0.10X1 + 0.55X2 + 0.70X3 >= 0
CON4:        -0.15X1 + 0.30X2 + 0.45X3 <= 0
CON5:        -0.10X1 + 0.50X2 + 0.80X3 >= 0
CON6:        -0.25X1 + 0.35X2 + 0.65X3 <= 0
CON7:        -0.05X1 + 0.15X2 + 0.91X3 >= 0
CON8:        -0.15X1 + 0.05X2 + 0.81X3 <= 0
CON9:        -0.02X1 + 0.01X2 + 0.72X3 >= 0
CON10:       -0.08X1 - 0.05X2 + 0.66X3 <= 0
CON11:            X1 +     X2 +     X3 = 95
CON12:
-->   NONE
-->   SOLVE


OBJECTIVE FUNCTION ATTAINS A MINIMUM VALUE OF 2608.662 AT:
              X2 =         12.23
              X3 =          2.40
              X1 =         80.37

-->   STOP
```

Display 3.1. Mixan Blends' initial problem.


```
#
RUN $DELIBR/LP
#RUNNING 9141
TYPE HELP IF YOU NEED IT
-->   #?
LOAD
ENTER OBJECTIVE FUNCTION:
OBJ*FN: MIN    27X1 +    29X2 +    35X3
ENTER CONSTRAINTS:
CON1:         0.15X1 + 0.55X2'+ 0.55X3 '>= 0
CON2:        -0.10X1 + 0.30X2 + 0.30X3 <= 0
CON3:         0.15X1 + 0.60X2 + 0.75X3 >= 0
CON4:        -0.05X1 + 0.40X2 + 0.55X3 <= 0
CON5:        -0.10X1 + 0.50X2 + 0.80X3 >= 0
CON6:        -0.25X1 + 0.35X2 + 0.65X3 <= 0
CON7:        -0.05X1 + 0.15X2 + 0.91X3 >= 0
CON8:        -0.15X1 + 0.05X2 + 0.81X3 <= 0
CON9:        -0.02X1 + 0.01X2 + 0.72X3 >= 0
CON10:       -0.08X1 - 0.05X2 + 0.66X3 <= 0
CON11:            X1 +     X2 +     X3 = 95
CON12:
-->   NONE
-->   SOLVE
CONSTRAINTS ARE TOO RESTRICTIVE
PROBLEM CANNOT BE SOLVED

-->   STOP
```

Display 3.2. Mixan Blends' problem with revised constraints (CON 3 and CON 4 revised).

selected. Therefore, it is helpful to include in the initial formulation as many sources of material as practicable. The linear programming solution will always choose the most economical sources.

It was convenient to assume that the handling and blending costs in Mixan Blends' case were $10 per ton, regardless of the quantity or quality of aggregate. Of course, that cost will usually vary, as in Packet-Down's situation considered next.

3.3. PACKET-DOWN'S PROBLEM

Packet-Down Highway Contractors, Inc., is building a roadway which requires 1000 cubic yards (about 2000 tons) of grade A1 gravel for the base course and another 750 cubic yards (about 1500 tons) for the subbase. Usually, Packet-Down obtains needed roadway materials from natural earth deposits which require on-site processing (including blending) to meet contract specifications. This time there are three quarries within proximity of the roadway site (see Figure 3.1). The material from each of these quarries is acceptable to the local highway department, except for the gradation and plasticity-index requirements (see Table 3.3). The material characteristics and unit prices of each appear in Table 3.4. In addition, Packet-Down has contracted with a trucker to haul materials to the job site for $0.12 per ton-mile. On-site processing costs are typically about 40¢ per ton of quarry material.

Packet-Down can also obtain commercially preblended grade A1 gravel requiring no on-site processing. The unit price and material characteristics of this preblended gravel appear in Table 3.5. While this commercial mix is costlier, the price includes preprocessing and delivery.

The data show that no one of the quarries can provide material that meets gradation and plasticity-index requirements. Packet-Down's managers seek the most economical means of obtaining the required roadway material.

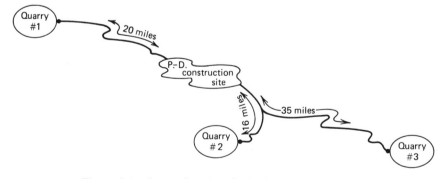

Figure 3.1.   Quarry locations for Packet-Down's roadway.

TABLE 3.3. Contract Specifications

Gradation:	Sieve Size	Percent Passing
	1 inch	100% (by weight)
	$\frac{1}{2}$ inch	65–100%
	No. 4	40–60%
	No. 40	15–25%
	No. 200	5–15%
Plasticity Index:	\multicolumn{2}{l}{The plasticity index (PI) of material passing the No. 40 sieve shall be from 4 to 10% for subbase construction only.}

Plasticity Index: The plasticity index (PI) of material passing the No. 40 sieve shall be from 4 to 10% for subbase construction only.

TABLE 3.4. Material Characteristics

| Deposits | \multicolumn{5}{c}{Percent Passing Each Sieve Size (by weight)} | Plasticity Index (PI) | Cost ($/ton) |
	1 inch	$\frac{1}{2}$ inch	No. 4	No. 40	No. 200		
Quarry I	100	95	50	30	12	14.8	2.80
Quarry II	100	95	85	20	10	3.5	3.10
Quarry III	100	85	65	10	5.5	2.0	3.50

TABLE 3.5. Commercial Blend Data

| | \multicolumn{5}{c}{Percent Passing Each Sieve Size (by weight)} | Plasticity Index (PI) | Cost ($/ton) |
	1 inch	$\frac{1}{2}$ inch	No. 4	No. 40	No. 200		
Commercial Blend	100	80	50	20	7	7.0	7.00

3.4. FORMULATING PACKET-DOWN'S PROBLEM

If Packet-Down continues its practice of purchasing only natural deposits and blending on site, it might formulate a linear programming problem similar to Mixan Blends' in Section 3.2. That is, let X_1, X_2, and X_3 be the quantity of material (in tons) from the respective quarries for the base course. Similarly, let Y_1, Y_2, and Y_3 denote the number of tons of materials for the subbase course.

For the objective equation we need the unit costs of purchasing, hauling, and processing each of the deposits. For material from Quarry I, these costs are, respectively, $2.80, $0.12 \times 20 = 2.40 for the 20-mile haul, and $0.40, for a total of $5.60 per ton. Similar calculations for the other two quarries yield $5.42 per ton and $8.10 per ton, respectively. Therefore, the objective equation is:

$$\text{minimize:} \quad Z = \$5.60(X_1 + Y_1) + 5.42(X_2 + Y_2) + 8.10(X_3 + Y_3)$$

To satisfy the roadway quantity requirements, include the constraints:

$$X_1 + X_2 + X_3 \geq 2000 \text{ tons (of base course)}$$

$$Y_1 + Y_2 + Y_3 \geq 1500 \text{ tons (of subbase)}$$

Each of the natural deposits are satisfactory for 1-inch and $\frac{1}{2}$-inch sieve sizes individually. Therefore, they are satisfactory in any combination, and no constraints are needed for these gradation limits. The same is true for the No. 200 sieve size. However, constraints are necessary to meet the gradation requirements for the No. 4 and No. 40 sieve sizes. These are formulted similar to those in the Mixan Blends' example. The result is:

$$\left.\begin{array}{l} 0.10X_1 + 0.45X_2 + 0.25X_3 \geq 0 \\ -0.10X_1 + 0.25X_2 + 0.05X_3 \leq 0 \\ 0.10Y_1 + 0.45Y_2 + 0.25Y_3 \geq 0 \\ -0.10Y_1 + 0.25Y_2 + 0.05Y_3 \leq 0 \end{array}\right\} \quad \text{No. 4 sieve}$$

$$\left.\begin{array}{l} 0.15X_1 + 0.05X_2 - 0.05X_3 \geq 0 \\ 0.05X_1 - 0.05X_2 - 0.15X_3 \leq 0 \\ 0.15Y_1 + 0.05Y_2 - 0.05Y_3 \geq 0 \\ 0.05Y_1 - 0.05Y_2 - 0.15Y_3 \leq 0 \end{array}\right\} \quad \text{No. 40 sieve}$$

Only the plasticity-index requirement remains to be considered. A rule that the plasticity index of a mixture is a weighted average of the plasticity indices of its components is expressed by:

$$\text{PI}_{\text{mixture}} = \frac{(\text{PI})_1 f_1 Y_1 + (\text{PI})_2 f_2 Y_2 + (\text{PI})_3 f_3 Y_3}{f_1 Y_1 + f_2 Y_2 + f_3 Y_3}$$

where $f_1, f_2,$ and f_3 are the respective fractions of each material which pass the No. 40 sieve; and $(\text{PI})_1, (\text{PI})_2,$ and $(\text{PI})_3$ are the plasticity indices of each deposit. Since the contract specifies that the plasticity index of the mixture be between 4 and 10%, write:

$$4(\%) \leq \frac{14.8(0.3)Y_1 + 3.5(0.2)Y_2 + 2.0(0.1)Y_3}{0.3Y_1 + 0.2Y_2 + 0.1Y_3} \leq 10(\%)$$

This can be rewritten as the subbase placticity-index requirement:

$$3.24Y_1 - 0.10Y_2 - 0.20Y_3 \geq 0$$

and

$$1.44Y_1 - 1.30Y_2 - 0.80Y_3 \leq 0$$

These two final constraints, together with the nonnegativity condition and the assumption that only natural earth deposits are used, complete the formulation of Packet-Down's problem.

The computer-aided solution is:

$$Z^* = \$22{,}506.54$$

$$X_1 = 1272.73, \qquad X_2 = 454.55, \qquad X_3 = 272.73$$

$$Y_1 = 542.90, \qquad Y_2 = 32.17, \qquad Y_3 = 924.93$$

as shown in Display 3.3. A simple hand calculation shows that the total cost of the base course mixture is \$11,800.01 (or \$5.90 per ton), while that of the subbase is \$10,706.53 (or \$7.13 per ton).

Clearly, it is economical for Packet-Down to purchase the commercial mix for the subbase since its unit price of \$7.00 per ton is 13¢ per ton less than that of the least-cost subbase mix from natural deposits. The unit

```
#
RUN $DELIBR/LP
#RUNNING 8639
TYPE HELP IF YOU NEED IT
-->  #?
LOAD
ENTER OBJECTIVE FUNCTION:
OBJ*FN: MIN  5.60X1 + 5.42X2 + 8.10X3 + 5.60Y1 + 5.42Y2 + 8.10Y3
ENTER CONSTRAINTS:
CON1:          X1 +      X2 +      X3 >= 2000
CON2:       0.10X1 + 0.45X2 + 0.25X3 >=   0
CON3:      -0.10X1 + 0.25X2 + 0.05X3 <=   0
CON4:       0.15X1 + 0.05X2 - 0.05X3 >=   0
CON5:       0.05X1 - 0.05X2 - 0.15X3 <=   0
CON6:          Y1 +      Y2 +      Y3 >= 1500
CON7:       0.10Y1 + 0.45Y2 + 0.25Y3 >=   0
CON8:      -0.10Y1 + 0.25Y2 + 0.05Y3 <=   0
CON9:       0.15Y1 + 0.05Y2 - 0.05Y3 >=   0
CON10:      0.05Y1 - 0.05Y2 - 0.15Y3 <=   0
CON11:      3.24Y1 - 0.10Y2 - 0.20Y3 >=   0
CON12:      1.44Y1 - 1.30Y2 - 0.80Y3 <=   0
CON13:
-->  NONE
-->  SOLVE

OBJECTIVE FUNCTION ATTAINS A MINIMUM VALUE OF 22506.542 AT:
          X2 =              454.55
          X1 =             1272.73
          X3 =              272.73
          Y2 =               32.17
          Y1 =              542.90
          Y3 =              924.93

-->  STOP
```

Display 3.3. Packet-Down's initial formulation and solution.

price of commercial blend is also less than the total unit cost of Quarry III material. Thus it may be cheaper to mix some of the commercial blend with natural deposits.

To investigate the latter possibility, revise the formulation as follows. Let X_c and Y_c be the respective amounts of commercial material used directly as base and subbase courses, and let X_4 and Y_4 be the respective amounts of commercial material to blend with natural earth deposits.

A revised objective equation is:

minimize:

$$Z = \$5.60(X_1 + Y_1) + \$5.42(X_2 + Y_2) + 8.10(X_3 + Y_3)$$
$$+ \$7.40(X_4 + Y_4) + \$7.00(X_c + Y_c)$$

The coefficient $\$7.40$ of X_4 and Y_4 includes the 40¢ per ton processing cost.

The quantity constraints become:

$$(X_1 + X_2 + X_3 + X_4) + X_c \geq 2000$$

and

$$(Y_1 + Y_2 + Y_3 + Y_4) + Y_c \geq 1500$$

To maintain the gradation integrity of the base course mix for the No. 4 sieve, write:

$$0.40 \leq \frac{0.50X_1 + 0.85X_2 + 0.65X_3 + 0.50X_4}{X_1 + X_2 + X_3 + X_4} \leq 0.60$$

and for the No. 40 sieve:

$$0.15 \leq \frac{0.30X_1 + 0.20X_2 + 0.10X_3 + 0.20X_4}{X_1 + X_2 + X_3 + X_4} \leq 0.25$$

Similar constraints are required for the subbase course. In addition, the plasticity-index constraints become:

$$4 \leq \frac{14.8(0.3)Y_1 + 3.5(0.2)Y_2 + 2.0(0.1)Y_3 + 7.0(0.2)Y_4}{0.3Y_1 + 0.2Y_2 + 0.1Y_3 + 0.2Y_4} \leq 10$$

Each of the constraints are rewritten in Display 3.4. The computer-aided solution yields:

$$Z^* = \$20,992.61$$

and

$$X_1 = 1272.73, \quad X_2 = 454.55, \quad X_3 = 272.73, \quad X_4 = X_c = 0$$

$$Y_1 = 588.24, \quad Y_2 = 428.57, \quad Y_3 = 0, \quad Y_4 = 483.19, \quad Y_c = 0$$

Indeed, it is cheaper to use the commercial blend in the mixture for the subbase, but not in the base course. A sensitivity analysis would show

```
#
RUN $DELIBR/LP
#RUNNING 8685
TYPE HELP IF YOU NEED IT
-->  #?
LOAD
ENTER OBJECTIVE FUNCTION:
OBJ*FN: MIN    5.60X1 + 5.42X2 + 8.10X3 + 7.40X4 + 7.00XC,
              +5.60Y1 + 5.42Y2 + 8.10Y3 + 7.40Y4 + 7.00YC
ENTER CONSTRAINTS:
CON1:         X1 +     X2 +     X3 +     X4 +     XC >= 2000
CON2:     0.10X1 + 0.45X2 + 0.25X3 + 0.10X4 >=  0
CON3:    -0.10X1 + 0.25X2 + 0.05X3 - 0.10X4 <=  0
CON4:     0.15X1 + 0.05X2 - 0.05X3 + 0.05X4 >=  0
CON5:     0.05X1 - 0.05X2 - 0.15X3 - 0.05X4 <=  0
CON6:         Y1 +     Y2 +     Y3 +     Y4 +     YC >= 1500
CON7:     0.10Y1 + 0.45Y2 + 0.25Y3 + 0.10Y4 >=  0
CON8:    -0.10Y1 + 0.25Y2 + 0.05Y3 - 0.10Y4 <=  0
CON9:     0.15Y1 + 0.05Y2 - 0.05Y3 + 0.05Y4 >=  0
CON10:    0.05Y1 - 0.05Y2 - 0.15Y3 - 0.05Y4 <=  0
CON11:    3.24Y1 - 0.10Y2 - 0.20Y3 + 0.60Y4 >=  0
CON12:    1.44Y1 - 1.30Y2 - 0.80Y3 - 0.60Y4 <=  0
CON13:
-->  NONE
-->  SOLVE

OBJECTIVE FUNCTION ATTAINS A MINIMUM VALUE OF 20992.605 AT:
            X2 =        454.55
            X1 =       1272.73
            X3 =        272.73
            Y2 =        428.57
            Y1 =        588.24
            Y4 =        483.19

      ALL OTHER VARIABLES HAVE A VALUE OF ZERO.

-->  STOP
```

Display 3.4. Packet-Down's problem with provision for commercial blend.

that if the price of the commercial mix were reduced to $6.83 per ton or less, it would be economical to use this material in both the base and the subbase mixes (in lieu of Quarry III material). Further, if the commercial blend were priced lower than $5.71 per ton, it would make a more economical subbase than any possible mixture of the four aggregate sources. Display 3.5 shows that if the commercial blend were $5.64 per ton (or less), Packet-Down could save money on its base and subbase material requirements using only the commercial blend, that is:

$$X_c = 2000, \qquad Y_c = 1500, \qquad \text{and} \qquad Z^* = \$19{,}740$$

Now suppose that the quantity of commercial material is limited to 1600 cubic yards and its purchase price (including delivery) is $5.70 per cubic yard. The previous formulation can be revised by simply changing the cost coefficients of the commercial blend variables X_4, X_c, Y_4, and Y_c

```
#
RUN $DELIBR/LP
#RUNNING 8726
TYPE HELP IF YOU NEED IT
-->  #?
LOAD
ENTER OBJECTIVE FUNCTION:
OBJ*FN: MIN   5.60X1 + 5.42X2 + 8.10X3 + 6.04X4 + 5.64XC,
             +5.60Y1 + 5.42Y2 + 8.10Y3 + 6.04Y4 + 5.64YC
ENTER CONSTRAINTS:
CON1:           X1 +    X2 +    X3 +    X4 +        XC >= 2000
CON2:        0.10X1 + 0.45X2 + 0.25X3 + 0.10X4 >=  0
CON3:       -0.10X1 + 0.25X2 + 0.05X3 - 0.10X4 <=  0
CON4:        0.15X1 + 0.05X2 - 0.05X3 + 0.05X4 >=  0
CON5:        0.05X1 - 0.05X2 - 0.15X3 - 0.05X4 <=  0
CON6:           Y1 +    Y2 +    Y3 +    Y4 +        YC >= 1500
CON7:        0.10Y1 + 0.45Y2 + 0.25Y3 + 0.10Y4 >=  0
CON8:       -0.10Y1 + 0.25Y2 + 0.05Y3 - 0.10Y4 <=  0
CON9:        0.15Y1 + 0.05Y2 - 0.05Y3 + 0.05Y4 >=  0
CON10:       0.05Y1 - 0.05Y2 - 0.15Y3 - 0.05Y4 <=  0
CON11:       3.24Y1 - 0.10Y2 - 0.20Y3 + 0.60Y4 >=  0
CON12:       1.44Y1 - 1.30Y2 - 0.80Y3 - 0.60Y4 <=  0
CON13:
-->  NONE
-->  SOLVE


OBJECTIVE FUNCTION ATTAINS A MINIMUM VALUE OF 19740 AT:

            XC =      2000.00
            YC =      1500.00

     ALL OTHER VARIABLES HAVE A VALUE OF ZERO.

-->  STOP
```

Display 3.5. Packet-Down's problem with commercial blend and revised cost coefficients.

and including the quantity constraint:

$$X_4 + X_c + Y_4 + Y_c \leq 1600 \text{ (cubic yards)}$$

The revised formulation appears in Display 3.6 with the solution:

$$Z^* = \$19,866.10$$

$$X_1 = 1000.00, \quad X_2 = 571.43, \quad X_3 = 0, \quad X_4 = 428.57, \quad X_c = 0$$

$$Y_1 = 190.08, \quad Y_2 = 138.49, \quad Y_3 = 0, \quad Y_4 = 156.14,$$

$$Y_c = 1015.29$$

The limited supply of commercial material should be used in the base course mix, and in both mixed and unmixed forms as subbase.

This example illustrates the skill required to formulate blending-type problems. When both input costs vary (with usage) and material quantities are limited, the least-cost solution may involve using some materials in more than one way. Therefore, separate decision variables are needed for each usage. In this case, the most economical solution uses the commercial blend in a combination mix ($Y_4 = 156.14$) as subbase over

```
#
RUN $DELIBR/LP
#RUNNING 8761
TYPE HELP IF YOU NEED IT
--> #?
LOAD
ENTER OBJECTIVE FUNCTION:
OBJ*FN: MIN  5.60X1 + 5.42X2 + 8.10X3 + 6.10X4 + 5.70XC,
            +5.60Y1 + 5.42Y2 + 8.10Y3 + 6.10Y4 + 5.70YC
ENTER CONSTRAINTS:
CON1:             X1 +     X2 +     X3 +     X4 +     XC >= 2000
CON2:         0.10X1 + 0.45X2 + 0.25X3 + 0.10X4 >=  0
CON3:        -0.10X1 + 0.25X2 + 0.05X3 - 0.10X4 <=  0
CON4:         0.15X1 + 0.05X2 - 0.05X3 + 0.05X4 >=  0
CON5:         0.05X1 - 0.05X2 - 0.15X3 - 0.05X4 <=  0
CON6:             Y1 +     Y2 +     Y3 +     Y4 +     YC >= 1500
CON7:         0.10Y1 + 0.45Y2 + 0.25Y3 + 0.10Y4 >=  0
CON8:        -0.10Y1 + 0.25Y2 + 0.05Y3 - 0.10Y4 <=  0
CON9:         0.15Y1 + 0.05Y2 - 0.05Y3 + 0.05Y4 >=  0
CON10:        0.05Y1 - 0.05Y2 - 0.15Y3 - 0.05Y4 <=  0
CON11:        3.24Y1 - 0.10Y2 - 0.20Y3 + 0.60Y4 >=  0
CON12:        1.44Y1 - 1.30Y2 - 0.80Y3 - 0.60Y4 <=  0
CON13:            X4 +     XC +     Y4 +     YC <= 1600
CON14:
-->  NONE
-->  SOLVE


OBJECTIVE FUNCTION ATTAINS A MINIMUM VALUE OF 19866.099 AT:
                X2 =       571.43
                X1 =      1000.00
                X4 =       428.57
                Y2 =       138.49
                Y1 =       190.08
                YC =      1015.29
                Y4 =       156.14

     ALL OTHER VARIABLES HAVE A VALUE OF ZERO.

-->  STOP
```

Display 3.6. Packet-Down's problem with a limited quantity of commercial blend.

one stretch of roadway and unmixed ($Y_c = 1015.29$) over another. Similar results may occur when capacity constraints are relevant, such as when there are limitations on the amount of material that may be processed in a given time or by a particular machine.

3.5. A FINAL COMMENT

There is an understandable temptation to review the formulation of a linear programming problem and remove constraints that are redundant or seemingly unnecessary. For example, the first gradation constraint in Displays 3.1 and 3.2,

$$0.15X_1 + 0.55X_2 + 0.55X_3 \geq 0, \quad \tfrac{3}{8}\text{-inch sieve}$$

will obviously be satisfied since all coefficients are positive and the variables X_1, X_2, and X_3 cannot have negative values. Therefore, solutions will not be affected if that constraint is omitted. While such an omission cannot be faulted, it is better practice to resist the temptation. If data should change, the omitted constraint could become viable. Suppose, for example, that Supplier I revises the gradation proportions of his aggregate. Specifically, suppose that the percentage passing the $\frac{3}{8}$-inch sieve is reduced to 40. The coefficient of X_1 in the above constraint should be changed to -0.05, and the constraint is viable. Its omission could cause one to accept an incorrect solution. The added computational cost of a constraint or two is apt to be minor as compared with the effort and distraction of remembering that some constraints were omitted in an earlier use of the formulation and that they should be checked for inclusion now.

CHAPTER 4

MINIMIZING EARTHMOVING COSTS

Overhill and Dale, a roadway grading contractor, is preparing to alter the terrain for a proposed roadway. Figure 4.1 shows profiles of the desired roadway and the original terrain. The roadway is divided into nine 1000-foot sections with the estimated cut and fill quantities indicated for each section. For example, 20,000 cubic yards of cut are required in section 1; 30,000 cubic yards of fill for section 2; 20,000 cubic yards of cut in section 3; and so on. Two relevant managerial questions are, of course, how much earth should be moved and from where to where, so that earthmoving costs are a minimum.

This chapter develops a modern and versatile method based upon linear programming for answering these questions of how much? and where? Before developing this new method, it is useful to consider some earthwork economics and the conventional mass diagram method for earthwork distribution.

In general, earthwork operations involve three categories of cost:

1. Excavation and loading.
2. Haul.
3. Placement and compaction.

For fixed quantities of cut and fill, the costs of excavation (including loading) and placement (including compaction) are typically proportional to the earthwork quantities. The cost of haul, however, is proportional to both the earthwork quantities and the haul distances. The customary unit of haul is the *station-yard* (abbreviated sta-yd), defined as the movement of 1 cubic yard of material through a distance of 1 station. Hence, for a given quantity of earth to be moved, the costs of excavation and placement are fixed, and the economic distribution of cut and fill is the one that minimizes the total haul. The conventional mass diagram is useful in these situations.

4.1. MASS DIAGRAM METHOD

A *mass diagram* is a graphic representation of the cumulative volume of earth along the roadway (after adjustments for swell and/or shrinkage). The mass diagram for the planned roadway of Overhill and Dale's project (Figure 4.1) is shown in Figure 4.2. The difference in vertical heights of the mass curve between successive stations is the amount of cut (if positive) or fill (if negative) between the two stations. Hence, the value of the curve is zero at station 0; it increases to 20 at station 1 (because of the available cut in Section 1); it decreases to -10 at station 2 (because of the fill requirement in section 2); it increases to $+10$ at station 3 (because of the available cut in section 3); and so on.

Two useful properties of the mass diagram are:

1. A horizontal line which intersects the mass diagram in two or more points (lines *MN* and *PQ* in Figure 4.2 are examples) indicates equal amounts of cut and fill between points of intersection. Such a line is called a *balancing line,* and its end points are *balancing points.*
2. The area between a balancing line and the mass curve is equal to the haul (in station-yards) resulting from moving the available cut into the area of fill between the balancing points.

These two properties of the mass diagram determine the minimum amount of haul and, therefore (when haul costs are directly proportional to the distance traveled), the most economic distribution of cut and fill. Clearly, the *zero line* (abscissa) of Overhill and Dale's mass diagram (Figure 4.2) is a balancing line for the entire roadway. Also, cut and fill quantities are equal between point A (station 0) and point B, between points B and C, between, C and D, between points D and E, and between points E and F (station 9). The arrows in Figure 4.3 indicate how cut should be distributed in sections of fill based upon this balancing line. For simplicity, the volumes of earth in cut and fill were assumed to be unchanged by the movement from their original positions. The next chapter deals with the effect of volume changes.

Note that the mass diagram method does not tell which material to move from one section to another. It only provides guidelines. For example, as shown in Figure 4.3, the 10,000 cubic yards of cut in section 7 could be used as fill in either section 8 or section 9. The other section would be filled from cut in section 6. There is (theoretically) no preference between these alternative possibilities chosen with the aid of the mass diagram.

The (approximate) areas of each loop between the zero balancing line and the mass curve were determined graphically and are shown in parentheses on the mass diagram in Figure 4.3. If excavation (including loading) costs are estimated as 50¢ per cubic yard, haul costs at 10¢ per station-yard, and placement (including compaction) at $1.00 per cubic

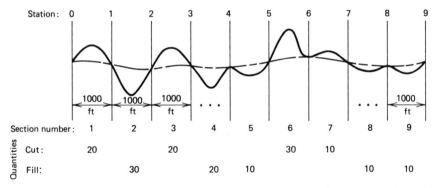

Figure 4.1. Road profile with estimated quantities of cut and fill. Quantities in thousands of cubic yards.

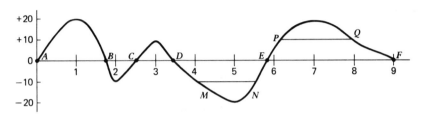

Figure 4.2. Mass diagram: Overhill and Dale's project.

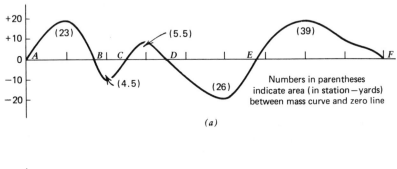

(a)

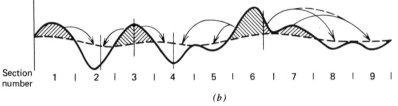

(b)

Figure 4.3. Distribution of cut and fill based upon mass diagram. (a) Mass diagram. (b) Distribution.

yard, the total earthmoving cost is:

$$EC = (\$0.50 \times 80{,}000) + (\$0.10 \times 98{,}000) + (\$1.00 \times 80{,}000)$$
$$= \$129{,}800$$

where 80,000 represents the quantities of excavation and placement, and 98,000 is the total haul (equal to the sum of the loop areas in Figure 4.3).

The mass diagram approach outlined above can provide some answers to the questions of how much? and where? However, the quality of the answers (and, hence, their usefulness) diminishes in such practical situations as the following:

1. When hauling costs are not directly proportional to the haul distance.
2. When soil characteristics vary along the roadway (particularly the percentages of swell or shrinkage).
3. When additional quantities of soil are available, or may be disposed of, at off-the-roadway sites.

These comments are not intended to discourage use of the mass diagram, but to indicate its limitations and to motivate discussion of a more powerful method.

4.2. LINEAR PROGRAMMING METHOD

To formulate a linear program for the distribution of earthwork quantities, begin by labeling the unknown quantities of earth to be moved between sections of roadway. Let $X(i,j)$ represent the (to be determined) quantities of earth (in appropriate units) to be moved from section i to section j for each value of i and j. For Overhill and Dale's problem, the variables (in thousands of cubic yards) are:

$$X(1,2), \quad X(1,4), \quad X(1,5), \quad X(1,8), \quad X(1,9)$$
$$X(3,2), \quad X(3,4), \quad X(3,5), \quad X(3,8), \quad X(3,9)$$
$$X(6,2), \quad X(6,4), \quad X(6,5), \quad X(6,8), \quad X(6,9)$$
$$X(7,2), \quad X(7,4), \quad X(7,5), \quad X(7,8), \quad X(7,9)$$

These 20 variables correspond to every possible pair of cut and fill sections. Note that variables such as $X(1,3)$ and $X(2,4)$, for example, are not listed since there is no advantage in moving quantities of earth to roadway sections requiring only cut (as in section 3), or from sections requiring only fill (as in section 2).

The total cost of earthwork can be obtained by multiplying the earthwork quantities $X(i,j)$ by their unit costs and adding them for all pairs of sections. For example, the unit cost of moving earth from section 1 to section 2 is:

$$0.50(\$/\text{yd}^3) + 0.10(\$/\text{sta-yd}) \times 1(\text{station}) + 1.00(\$/\text{yd}^3) = 1.60(\$/\text{yd}^3)$$
(excavation)   (haul)   (placement)

or \$1600 per thousand cubic yards. Similarly, the unit cost coefficient for variable $X(1,4)$ is:

$$0.50(\$/\text{yd}^3) + 0.10(\$/\text{sta-yd}) \times 3(\text{stations}) + 1.00(\$/\text{yd}^3) = 1.80(\$/\text{yd}^3)$$

or \$1800 per thousand cubic yards.

Note that the haul cost has been approximated by the product of the unit haul cost (\$0.10 per station yard) and the approximate distance (in stations) between centers of gravity of the cut and fill quantities. The unit costs for the other variables are determined similarly.

Overhill and Dale's objective can then be expressed as:

minimize:

$$\begin{aligned}
Z = {}& 1600X(1,2) + 1800X(1,4) + 1900X(1,5) + 2200X(1,8) \\
& + 2300X(1,9) + 1600X(3,2) + 1600X(3,4) + 1700X(3,5) \\
& + 2000X(3,8) + 2100X(3,9) + 1900X(6,2) + 1700X(6,4) \\
& + 1600X(6,5) + 1700X(6,8) + 1800X(6,9) + 2000X(7,2) \\
& + 1800X(7,4) + 1700X(7,5) + 1600X(7,8) + 1700X(7,9)
\end{aligned}$$

The formulation requires quantity constraints. Specifically, for sections of cut, the quantity of earth removed should equal the required cut. That is, for section 1:

$$X(1,2) + X(1,4) + X(1,5) + X(1,8) + X(1,9) = 20$$

and for sections 3, 6, and 7:

$$X(3,2) + X(3,4) + X(3,5) + X(3,8) + X(3,9) = 20$$
$$X(6,2) + X(6,4) + X(6,5) + X(6,8) + X(6,9) = 30$$
$$X(7,2) + X(7,4) + X(7,5) + X(7,8) + X(7,9) = 10$$

where all quantities are in thousands of cubic yards.

Similarly, for sections of fill, the quantity of earth moved into a section should equal the required fill. Therefore, for section 2:

$$X(1,2) + X(3,2) + X(6,2) + X(7,2) = 30$$

and for sections 4, 5, 8, and 9:

$$X(1,4) + X(3,4) + X(6,4) + X(7,4) = 20$$
$$X(1,5) + X(3,5) + X(6,5) + X(7,5) = 10$$
$$X(1,8) + X(3,8) + X(6,8) + X(7,8) = 10$$
$$X(1,9) + X(3,9) + X(6,9) + X(7,9) = 10$$

Of course, negative values of $X(i,j)$ make no sense; so there is the final requirement that

$$X(i,j) \geq 0, \qquad i = 1,3,6,7; j = 2,4,5,8,9$$

Both the objective equation and the constraints of Overhill and Dale's problem are linear; therefore, linear optimization methods may be used. The complete formulation appears in Display 4.1 with the solution $Z^* = \$131,000$. The distribution of cut and fill is illustrated in Figure 4.4. Note that this distribution is essentially the same as that obtained by the mass diagram method. The small difference in cost between the two methods is a result of approximations. This difference could be reduced by sectioning the roadway into smaller intervals. (This is suggested as a problem in Appendix 4.)

```
#
RUN $DELIBR/LP
#RUNNING 7376
TYPE HELP IF YOU NEED IT
-->  #?
LOAD
ENTER OBJECTIVE FUNCTION:
OBJ*FN: MIN   1600 X12 + 1800 X14 + 1900 X15 + 2200 X18 + 2300 X19 +,
              1600 X32 + 1600 X34 + 1700 X35 + 2000 X38 + 2100 X39 +,
              1900 X62 + 1700 X64 + 1600 X65 + 1700 X68 + 1800 X69 +,
              2000 X72 + 1800 X74 + 1700 X75 + 1600 X78 + 1700 X79
ENTER CONSTRAINTS:
CON1:              X12 + X14 + X15 + X18 + X19 = 20
CON2:              X32 + X34 + X35 + X38 + X39 = 20
CON3:              X62 + X64 + X65 + X68 + X69 = 30
CON4:              X72 + X74 + X75 + X78 + X79 = 10
CON5:              X12 + X32 + X62 + X72       = 30
CON6:              X14 + X34 + X64 + X74       = 20
CON7:              X15 + X35 + X65 + X75       = 10
CON8:              X18 + X38 + X68 + X78       = 10
CON9:              X19 + X39 + X69 + X79       = 10
CON10:
-->  NONE
-->  SENSITIVITY
-->  SOLVE

OBJECTIVE FUNCTION ATTAINS A MINIMUM VALUE OF 131000 AT:
                       X12 =        20.00
                       X32 =        10.00
                       X65 =        10.00
                       X78 =        10.00
                       X34 =        10.00
                       X69 =        10.00
                       X64 =        10.00

     ALL OTHER VARIABLES HAVE A VALUE OF ZERO.

SENSITIVITY ANALYSIS:

     X14 WILL ENTER THE SOLUTION IF ITS COST IS DECREASED TO 1600.
CURRENTLY THIS IS SET AT 1800.

     X15 WILL ENTER THE SOLUTION IF ITS COST IS DECREASED TO 1500.
CURRENTLY THIS IS SET AT 1900.

     X18 WILL ENTER THE SOLUTION IF ITS COST IS DECREASED TO 1600.
CURRENTLY THIS IS SET AT 2200.

     X19 WILL ENTER THE SOLUTION IF ITS COST IS DECREASED TO 1700.
CURRENTLY THIS IS SET AT 2300.

     X62 WILL ENTER THE SOLUTION IF ITS COST IS DECREASED TO 1700.
CURRENTLY THIS IS SET AT 1900.
```

```
     X35 WILL ENTER THE SOLUTION IF ITS COST IS DECREASED TO 1500.
CURRENTLY THIS IS SET AT 1700.

     X38 WILL ENTER THE SOLUTION IF ITS COST IS DECREASED TO 1600.
CURRENTLY THIS IS SET AT 2000.

     X39 WILL ENTER THE SOLUTION IF ITS COST IS DECREASED TO 1700.
CURRENTLY THIS IS SET AT 2100.

     X68 WILL ENTER THE SOLUTION IF ITS COST IS DECREASED.   CURRENTLY
THIS IS SET AT 1700.

     X72 WILL ENTER THE SOLUTION IF ITS COST IS DECREASED TO 1600.
CURRENTLY THIS IS SET AT 2000.

     X74 WILL ENTER THE SOLUTION IF ITS COST IS DECREASED TO 1600.
CURRENTLY THIS IS SET AT 1800.

     X75 WILL ENTER THE SOLUTION IF ITS COST IS DECREASED TO 1500.
CURRENTLY THIS IS SET AT 1700.

     X79 WILL ENTER THE SOLUTION IF ITS COST IS DECREASED.   CURRENTLY
THIS IS SET AT 1700.

 --> STOP
```

Display 4.1. Overhill and Dale's formulation and solution with sensitivity analysis.

The sensitivity analysis of Display 4.1 indicates that variables $X(6,8)$ and $X(7,9)$ will increase from their current value of zero if their unit cost coefficients decrease, even if the decrease is minute. This means that, with the current unit costs, at least one alternative solution exists yielding the same value of Z^*, with $X(6,8)$ and/or $X(7,9)$ positive. For example, the distribution:

$$X(1,2) = 20, \quad X(3,2) = 10, \quad X(3,4) = 10, \quad X(6,4) = 10$$
$$X(6,5) = 10, \quad X(6,8) = 10, \quad X(7,9) = 10$$

and all other variables equal to zero, also yields $Z^* = \$131{,}000$ and is, therefore, a multiple solution. As discussed in Chapter 2, multiple solutions provide an opportunity to choose the solution that takes better account of factors that were not included in the mathematical formulation. For example, the solution with $X(6,8) = X(7,9) = 10$ might be preferable because of greater consistency in haul distances. On the

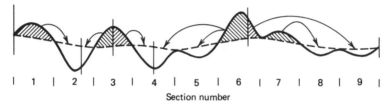

Figure 4.4. Optimal distribution of cut and fill by linear programming.

other hand, although haul costs are assumed to be directly proportional to distance, there may be advantages in longer (or shorter) stretches of haul so that the solution with $X(6, 9) = X(7, 8) = 10$ is preferred.

This formulation assumes that all cut is used as fill on the roadway, that is, no disposal of cut is permitted alongside the roadway. If such disposal is allowed, the equality signs of the cut constraints should be replaced with less-than-or-equal signs. Equivalently, additional variables such as $X(1, 1)$ and $X(3, 3)$ to represent the amount of roadside disposal should be included in the appropriate cut constraints. Of course, all earthmoving costs associated with roadside disposal must be considered. Similar remarks apply to the sections of fill. The following example considers such opportunities.

4.3. EARTHMOVING WITH BORROW PIT AND DISPOSAL OPPORTUNITIES

Figure 4.5 shows a profile view of a one-half-mile stretch of a proposed highway. The profile is divided into 100-foot sections, and cut and fill quantities are approximated. Excavation costs (including loading) are estimated as 30¢ per cubic yard, and placement costs (including compaction) at 90¢ per cubic yard. Unit haul costs are estimated at 6¢ per station-yard and are assumed constant along the highway.

A local contractor operates a borrow pit of 2500-cubic-yard capacity and will deliver additional fill anywhere along the roadway for 60¢ per cubic yard. The borrow material is expected to be well graded, and therefore, the estimated cost of its placement and compaction is only 70¢ per cubic yard. If material may be disposed of adjacent to the roadway at an estimated cost of 40¢ per cubic yard (including excavation, haul, and dumping), the questions of how much borrow material to purchase and for which sections of roadway are relevant.

The problem can be solved by either the mass diagram or the linear programming method. To use the latter, first identify the $X(i, j)$ variables, that is, the quantity (in hundreds of cubic yards) of earth to be moved from section i to section j, where i and j represent all sections of cut and fill, respectively. The sections of cut are 1 to 3, 7 to 11, and 19 to 22. Those of

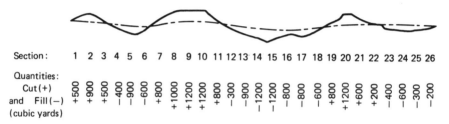

Figure 4.5. One-half-mile stretch of proposed highway (100-foot-long sections).

fill are 4 to 6, 12 to 18, and 23 to 26. Thus the variables are $X(1,4)$, $X(1,5), \ldots, X(1,26), X(2,4), \ldots, X(3,26), X(7,4), \ldots, X(11,26)$, $X(19,4), \ldots, X(22,25)$, and $X(22,26)$.

Since material may be procured from a commercial source and/or disposed of adjacent to the roadway, variables are needed to account for these possibilities. Define variables $X(B,j)$ as the quantity of borrow (in hundreds of cubic yards) to be purchased for section j, where $j = 4, 5, 6, 12, \ldots, 18, 23, \ldots, 26$. That is, $X(B, 4)$ is the amount of borrow (in hundreds of cubic yards) for use in section 4, and so on. Similarly, let $X(i,D)$ represent the amount of cut to be disposed alongside section i, where $i = 1, 2, 3, 7, \ldots, 11, 19, \ldots, 22$.

In total there are 194 variables — 168 representing the combinations of cut and fill, 14 borrow variables, and 12 disposal variables. While that number of variables is large by conventional standards, it is still small by computer-aided linear programming standards.

The unit cost for moving a cubic yard of soil between sections of cut and fill can be determined, as in the previous example, by summing the component unit costs for excavation, haul, and placement. For $X(1, 4)$, the unit earthmoving cost coefficient is approximated by

$$0.30(\$/\text{yd}^3) + 0.06(\$/\text{sta-yd}) \times 3(\text{stations}) + 0.90(\$/\text{yd}^3) = 1.38(\$/\text{yd}^3)$$

(excavation)   (haul)   (placement)   (total unit cost)

or \$138 per hundred cubic yards. Here the factor 3 is the approximate distance (in stations) between centers of gravity of cut (section 1) and fill (section 4). The unit costs for the remaining cut and fill variables are calculated similarly.

Since the contractor will deliver borrow material anywhere along the roadway at 60¢ per cubic yard, no specific haul charge is involved. Therefore, the unit cost of borrow will be constant along the roadway and equal to the sum of the purchase and placement costs, that is:

$$0.60(\$/\text{yd}^3) + 0.70(\$/\text{yd}^3) = 1.30(\$/\text{yd}^3)$$

or \$130 per hundred cubic yards, for all sections. The unit cost of \$40 per hundred cubic yards for disposing of material adjacent to the roadway is also constant. These unit costs (for all variables) are summarized in Table 4.1.

The objective equation to minimize total cost is written:

minimize:

$$Z = 138X(1,4) + 144X(1,5) + 150X(1,6) + 186X(1,12)$$
$$+ \cdots + 132X(22,24) + 138X(22,25) + 144X(22,26)$$
$$+ 40X(1,D) + \cdots + 40X(22,D) + 130X(B,4)$$
$$+ 130X(B,5) + \cdots + 130X(B,26)$$

TABLE 4.1. Unit Costs of Earthmoving ($/100 yds³)

Sections of Cut	\multicolumn{15}{c}{Sections of Fill}														
	4	5	6	12	13	14	15	16	17	18	23	24	25	26	D
1	138	144	150	186	192	198	204	210	216	222	252	258	264	270	40
2	132	138	144	180	186	192	198	204	210	216	246	252	258	264	40
3	126	132	138	174	180	186	192	198	204	210	240	246	252	258	40
7	138	132	126	150	156	162	168	174	180	186	216	222	228	234	40
8	144	138	132	144	150	156	162	168	174	180	210	216	222	228	40
9	150	144	138	138	144	150	156	162	168	174	204	210	216	222	40
10	156	150	144	132	138	144	150	156	162	168	198	204	210	216	40
11	162	156	150	126	132	138	144	150	156	162	192	198	204	210	40
19	210	204	198	162	156	150	144	138	132	138	144	150	156	162	40
20	216	210	204	168	162	156	150	144	138	132	138	144	150	156	40
21	222	216	210	174	168	162	156	150	144	138	132	138	144	150	40
22	228	222	216	180	174	168	162	156	150	144	126	132	138	144	40
B	130	130	130	130	130	130	130	130	130	130	130	130	130	130	●

There are 12 cut constraints, that is, one for each section of cut. For section 1:

$$X(1,4) + X(1,5) + X(1,6) + X(1,12) + X(1,13) + X(1,14)$$
$$+ X(1,15) + X(1,16) + X(1,17) + X(1,18) + X(1,23)$$
$$+ X(1,24) + X(1,25) + X(1,26) + X(1,D) = 5$$

and so on for the other eleven sections.

A constraint is required for each of the 14 sections of fill. For section 4:

$$X(1,4) + X(2,4) + X(3,4) + X(7,4) + X(8,4) + X(9,4)$$
$$+ X(10,4) + X(11,4) + X(19,4) + X(20,4) + X(21,4)$$
$$+ X(22,4) + X(B,4) = 4$$

and so on.

The capacity limitation on the borrow pit can be expressed as:

$$X(B,4) + X(B,5) + X(B,6) + X(B,12) + X(B,13) + X(B,14)$$
$$+ X(B,15) + X(B,16) + X(B,17) + X(B,18) + X(B,23)$$
$$+ X(B,24) + X(B,25) + X(B,26) \leq 25$$

where, of course, 25 is the limit of available borrow (in hundreds of cubic yards). Finally, each $X(i,j)$, $X(i,D)$, and $X(B,j)$ must be nonnegative (≥ 0). The complete formulation, involving 194 variables and 27 constraints, is shown in Table 4.2

TABLE 4.2. Objective and Constraints for the Contractor's Decision

```
OBJECTIVE FUNCTION:

MINIMIZE Z = 138X(1,4) + 144X(1,5) + 150X(1,6) + 186X(1,12) + 192X(1,13)
           + 198X(1,14) + 204X(1,15) + 210X(1,16) + 216X(1,17)
           + 222X(1,18) + 252X(1,23) + 258X(1,24) + 264X(1,25)
           + 270X(1,26) + 40X(1,D) + 132X(2,4) + 138X(2,5) + 144X(2,6)
           + 180X(2,12) + 186X(2,13) + 192X(2,14) + 198X(2,15)
           + 204X(2,16) + 210X(2,17) + 216X(2,18) + 246X(2,23)
           + 252X(2,24) + 258X(2,25) + 264X(2,26) + 40X(2,D) + 126X(3,14)
           + 132X(3,5) + 138X(3,6) + 174X(3,12) + 180X(3,13) + 186X(3,1)
           + 192X(3,15) + 198X(3,16) + 204X(3,17) + 210X(3,18)
           + 240X(3,23) + 246X(3,24) + 252X(3,25) + 258X(3,26) + 40X(3,D)
           + 138X(7,4) + 132X(7,5) + 126X(7,6) + 150X(7,12) + 156X(7,13)
           + 162X(7,14) + 168X(7,15) + 174X(7,16) + 180X(7,17)
           + 186X(7,18) + 216X(7,23) + 222X(7,24) + 228X(7,25)
           + 234X(7,26) + 40X(7,D) + 144X(8,4) + 138X(8,5) + 132X(8,6)
           + 144X(8,12) + 150X(8,13) + 156X(8,14) + 162X(8,15)
           + 168X(8,16) + 174X(8,17) + 180X(8,18) + 210X(8,23)
           + 216X(8,24) + 222X(8,25) + 228X(8,26) + 40X(8,D) + 150X(9,4)
           + 144X(9,5) + 138X(9,6) + 138X(9,12) + 144X(9,13) + 150X(9,14)
           + 156X(9,15) + 162X(9,16) + 168X(9,17) + 174X(9,18)
           + 204X(9,23) + 210X(9,24) + 216X(9,25) + 222X(9,26) + 40X(9,D)
           + 156X(10,4) + 150X(10,5) + 144X(10,6) + 132X(10,12)
           + 138X(10,13) + 144X(10,14) + 150X(10,15) + 156X(10,16)
           + 162X(10,17) + 168X(10,18) + 198X(10,23) + 204X(10,24)
           + 210X(10,25) + 216X(10,26) + 40X(10,D) + 162X(11,4)
           + 156X(11,5) + 150X(22,6) + 126X(11,12) + 132X(11,13)
           + 138X(11,14) + 144X(11,15) + 150X(11,16) + 156X(11,17)
           + 162X(11,18) + 192X(11,23) + 198X(11,24) + 204X(11,25)
           + 210X(11,26) + 40X(11,D) + 210X(19,4) + 204X(19,5)
           + 198X(19,6) + 162X(19,12) + 156X(19,13) + 150X(19,14)
           + 144X(19,15) + 138X(19,16) + 132X(19,17) + 126X(19,18)
           + 144X(19,23) + 150X(19,24) + 156X(19,25) + 162X(19,26)
           + 40X(19,D) + 216X(20,4) + 210X(20,5) + 204X(20,6)
           + 168X(20,12) + 162X(20,13) + 156X(20,14) + 150X(20,15)
           + 144X(20,16) + 138X(20,17) + 132X(20,18) + 138X(20,23)
           + 144X(20,24) + 150X(20,25) + 156X(20,26) + 40X(20,D)
           + 222X(21,4) + 216X(21,5) + 210X(21,6) + 174X(21,12)
           + 168X(21,13) + 162X(21,14) + 156X(21,15) + 150X(21,16)
           + 144X(21,17) + 138X(21,18) + 132X(21,23) + 138X(21,24)
           + 144X(21,25) + 150X(21,26) + 40X(21,D) + 228X(22,4)
           + 222X(22,5) + 216X(22,6) + 180X(22,12) + 174X(22,13)
           + 168X(22,14) + 162X(22,15) + 156X(22,16) + 150X(22,17)
           + 144X(22,18) + 126X(22,23) + 132X(22,24) + 138X(22,25)
           + 144X(22,26) + 40X(22,D) + 130X(B,4) + 130X(B,5) + 130X(B,6)
           + 130X(B,12) + 130X(B,13) + 130X(B,14) + 130X(B,15)
           + 130X(B,16) + 130X(B,17) + 130X(B,18) + 130X(B,23)
           + 130X(B,24) + 130X(B,25) + 130X(B,26)

CONSTRAINTS:

* CUT1:    X(1,4) + X(1,5) + X(1,6) + X(1,12) + X(1,13) + X(1,14) + X(1,15)
           + X(1,16) + X(1,17) + X(1,18) + X(1,23) + X(1,24) + X(1,25)
           + X(1,26) + X(1,D) = 5
* CUT2:    X(2,4) + X(2,5) + X(2,6) + X(2,12) + X(2,13) + X(2,14) + X(2,15)
           + X(2,16) + X(2,17) + X(2,18) + X(2,23) + X(2,24) + X(2,25)
           + X(2,26) + X(2,D) = 9
* CUT3:    X(3,4) + X(3,5) + X(3,6) + X(3,12) + X(3,13) + X(3,14) + X(3,15)
           + X(3,16) + X(3,17) + X(3,18) + X(3,23) + X(3,24) + X(3,25)
           + X(3,26) + X(3,D) = 5
* CUT7:    X(7,4) + X(7,5) + X(7,6) + X(7,12) + X(7,13) + X(7,14) + X(7,15)
           + X(7,16) + X(7,17) + X(7,18) + X(7,23) + X(7,24) + X(7,25)
           + X(7,26) + X(7,D) = 8
```

(Continued)

TABLE 4.2.   (Continued)

* CUT8:   X(8,4) + X(8,5) + X(8,6) + X(8,12) + X(8,13) + X(8,14) + X(8,15)
            + X(8,16) + X(8,17) + X(8,18) + X(8,23) + X(8,24) + X(8,25)
            + X(8,26) + X(8,D) =   10
* CUT9:   X(9,4) + X(9,5) + X(9,6) + X(9,12) + X(9,13) + X(9,14) + X(9,15)
            + X(9,16) + X(9,17) + X(9,18) + X(9,23) + X(9,24) + X(9,25)
            + X(9,26) + X(9,D) =   12
* CUT10:   X(10,4) + X(10,5) + X(10,6) + X(10,12) + X(10,13) + X(10,14)
            + X(10,15) + X(10,16) + X(10,17) + X(10,18) + X(10,23) + X(10,24)
            + X(10,25) + X(10,26) + X(10,D) =   12
* CUT11:   X(11,4) + X(11,5) + X(11,6) + X(11,12) + X(11,13) + X(11,14)
            + X(11,15) + X(11,16) + X(11,17) + X(11,18) + X(11,23) + X(11,24)
            + X(11,25) + X(11,26) + X(11,D) =   8
* CUT19:   X(19,4) + X(19,5) + X(19,6) + X(19,12) + X(19,13) + X(19,14)
            + X(19,15) + X(19,16) + X(19,17) + X(19,18) + X(19,23) + X(19,24)
            + X(19,25) + X(19,26) + X(19,D) =   8
* CUT20:   X(20,4) + X(20,5) + X(20,6) + X(20,12) + X(20,13) + X(20,14)
            + X(20,15) + X(20,16) + X(20,17) + X(20,18) + X(20,23) + X(20,24)
            + X(20,25) + X(20,26) + X(20,D) =   12
* CUT21:   X(21,4) + X(21,5) + X(21,6) + X(21,12) + X(21,13) + X(21,14)
            + X(21,15) + X(21,16) + X(21,17) + X(21,18) + X(21,23) + X(21,24)
            + X(21,25) + X(21,26) + X(21,D) =   6
* CUT22:   X(22,4) + X(22,5) + X(22,6) + X(22,12) + X(22,13) + X(22,14)
            + X(22,15) + X(22,16) + X(22,17) + X(22,18) + X(22,23) + X(22,24)
            + X(22,25) + X(22,26) + X(22,D) =   2
* FILL4:   X(B,4) + X(1,4) + X(2,4) + X(3,4) + X(7,4) + X(8,4) + X(9,4)
            + X(10,4) + X(11,4) + X(19,4) + X(20,4) + X(21,4) + X(22,4) =   4
* FILL5:   X(B,5) + X(1,5) + X(2,5) + X(3,5) + X(7,5) + X(8,5) + X(9,5)
            + X(10,5) + X(11,5) + X(19,5) + X(20,5) + X(21,5) + X(22,5) =   9
* FILL6:   X(B,6) + X(1,6) + X(2,6) + X(3,6) + X(7,6) + X(8,6) + X(9,6)
            + X(10,6) + X(11,6) + X(19,6) + X(20,6) + X(21,6) + X(22,6) =   6
* FILL12:   X(B,12) + X(1,12) + X(2,12) + X(3,12) + X(7,12) + X(8,12)
            + X(9,12) + X(10,12) + X(11,12) + X(19,12) + X(20,12) + X(21,12)
            + X(22,12) =   3
* FILL13:   X(B,13) + X(1,13) + X(2,13) + X(3,13) + X(7,13) + X(8,13)
            + X(9,13) + X(10,13) + X(11,13) + X(19,13) + X(20,13) + X(21,13)
            + X(22,13) =   9
* FILL14:   X(B,14) + X(1,14) + X(2,14) + X(3,14) + X(7,14) + X(8,14)
            + X(9,14) + X(10,14) + X(11,14) + X(19,14) + X(20,14) + X(21,14)
            + X(22,14) =   12
* FILL15:   X(B,15) + X(1,15) + X(2,15) + X(3,15) + X(7,15) + X(8,15)
            + X(9,15) + X(10,15) + X(11,15) + X(19,15) + X(20,15) + X(21,15)
            + X(22,15) =   12
* FILL16:   X(B,16) + X(1,16) + X(2,16) + X(3,16) + X(7,16) + X(8,16)
            + X(9,16) + X(10,16) + X(11,16) + X(19,16) + X(20,16) + X(21,16)
            + X(22,16) =   8
* FILL17:   X(B,17) + X(1,17) + X(2,17) + X(3,17) + X(7,17) + X(8,17)
            + X(9,17) + X(10,17) + X(11,17) + X(19,17) + X(20,17) + X(21,17)
            + X(22,17) =   8
* FILL18:   X(B,18) + X(1,18) + X(2,18) + X(3,18) + X(7,18) + X(8,18)
            + X(9,18) + X(10,18) + X(11,18) + X(19,18) + X(20,18) + X(21,18)
            + X(22,18) =   6
* FILL23:   X(B,23) + X(1,23) + X(2,23) + X(3,23) + X(7,23) + X(8,23)
            + X(9,23) + X(10,23) + X(11,23) + X(19,23) + X(20,23) + X(21,23)
            + X(22,23) =   4
* FILL24:   X(B,24) + X(1,24) + X(2,24) + X(3,24) + X(7,24) + X(8,24)
            + X(9,24) + X(10,24) + X(11,24) + X(19,24) + X(20,24) + X(21,14)
            + X(22,24) =   6
* FILL25:   X(B,25) + X(1,25) + X(2,25) + X(3,25) + X(7,25) + X(8,25)
            + X(9,25) + X(10,25) + X(11,25) + X(19,25) + X(20,25) + X(21,25)
            + X(22,25) =   3

TABLE 4.2.   (Continued)

* FILL26:	X(B,26) + X(1,26) + X(2,26) + X(3,26) + X(7,26) + X(8,26) + X(9,26) + X(10,26) + X(11,26) + X(19,26) + X(20,26) + X(21,26) + X(22,26) = 2
* CAPBP:	X(B,4) + X(B,5) + X(B,6) + X(B,12) + X(B,13) + X(B,14) + X(B,15) + X(B,16) + X(B,17) + X(B,18) + X(B,23) + X(B,24) + X(B,25) + X(B,26) <= 25

A portion of the computer output is shown in Display 4.2, and indicates that the minimum cost is $Z^* = \$13{,}224$. Recall, from Chapter 2, that the column headed ACTIVITY indicates the desired value of each $X(i,j)$. The REDUCED COST column provides additional sensitivity information, that is, the value in the latter column is a measure of the incremental increase in total cost if earth is moved between the corresponding sections of cut and fill. For example, the reduced cost of variable $X(1,4)$ is 6.00, and therefore, the value of Z would increase at least \$6.00 for each 100 cubic yards hauled between section 1 and section 4. The variable $X(2,4)$ equals zero in this solution, but its reduced cost also equals zero. Therefore, its value can be increased without changing the value of Z^*, that is, there is at least one alternate solution with $Z^* = \$13{,}224$ and $X(2,4)$ positive. There are 18 other variables which, like $X(2,4)$, equal zero in this solution, but are positive in one or more multiple solutions. These variables are indicated by an ★ in the final column. These alternate optimal solutions can be computed if needed. They are also obtainable using the mass diagram method. Incidentally, the computational cost of the computer-aided solution and sensitivity analysis for this problem was less than \$1.50.

4.4.   FORMULATING AN LP FOR EARTHMOVING

It is useful to review the linear programming formulations outlined in the previous two examples.

Problem.   Having a profile map of the existing terrain and the proposed roadway, the problem is to determine how much earth to move and from where to where to obtain the desired profile at minimum cost.

Cut and Fill Quantities.   First, determine the quantities of cut and fill required for each section of roadway.

Variables.   Next, define decision variables $X(i,j)$ for every pair of cut and fill sections. These variables represent the amount of cut to be hauled from section i to section j for each pair of values of i and j. Of course, the purpose of the analysis is to determine these amounts.

Excess material must be disposed of adjacent to the roadway or elsewhere. Define variables $X(i,D)$ as the amount of earth to be removed from section i and destined for the disposal site D. If there are several disposal sites, they can be distinguished by a notation such as $X(i, D1)$ and $X(i, D2)$, and so on. Any notation will do if it is convenient and unambiguous.

Similar remarks apply for borrow pits and sites. Let $X(B, j)$ denote borrow material to be placed in section j. Distinguish among several sources of borrow by using $X(B1, j)$ or $X(B2, j)$, and so on.

Costs.   Determine each $C(i, j)$, the net cost of moving a unit of earth from section i to section j. Each $C(i, j)$ is the sum of the unit costs of

NAME	ACTIVITY	REDUCED COST	NAME	ACTIVITY	REDUCED COST
COST	13224.00000	...			
X(1,4)	.	6.00000	X(8,4)	.	12.00000
X(1,5)	.	6.00000	X(8,5)	.	. *
X(1,6)	.	18.00000	X(8,6)	.	. *
X(1,12)	.	42.00000	X(8,12)	.	. *
X(1,13)	.	42.00000	X(8,13)	1.00000	.
X(1,14)	.	42.00000	X(8,14)	3.00000	.
X(1,15)	.	42.00000	X(8,15)	.	. *
X(1,16)	.	42.00000	X(8,16)	4.00000	.
X(1,17)	.	54.00000	X(8,17)	.	12.00000
X(1,18)	.	66.00000	X(8,18)	.	24.00000
X(1,23)	.	90.00000	X(8,23)	.	48.00000
X(1,24)	.	90.00000	X(8,24)	.	48.00000
X(1,25)	.	94.00000	X(8,25)	.	52.00000
X(1,26)	.	100.00000	X(8,26)	.	58.00000
X(1,D)	5.00000	.	X(8,D)	2.00000	.
X(2,4)	.	. *	X(9,4)	.	24.00000
X(2,5)	6.00000	.	X(9,5)	.	12.00000
X(2,6)	.	12.00000	X(9,6)	.	12.00000
X(2,12)	.	36.00000	X(9,12)	3.00000	.
X(2,13)	.	36.00000	X(9,13)	.	. *
X(2,14)	.	36.00000	X(9,14)	.	. *
X(2,15)	.	36.00000	X(9,15)	9.00000	.
X(2,16)	.	36.00000	X(9,16)	.	. *
X(2,17)	.	48.00000	X(9,17)	.	12.00000
X(2,18)	.	60,00000	X(9,18)	.	24.00000
X(2,23)	.	84.00000	X(9,23)	.	48.00000
X(2,24)	.	84.00000	X(9,24)	.	48.00000
X(2,25)	.	88.00000	X(9,25)	.	52.00000
X(2,26)	.	94.00000	X(9,26)	.	58.00000
X(2,D)	3.00000	.	X(9,D)	.	6.00000
X(3,4)	4.00000	.	X(10,4)	.	36.00000
X(3,5)	1.00000	.	X(10,5)	.	24.00000
X(3,6)	.	12.00000	X(10,6)	.	24.00000
X(3,12)	.	36.00000	X(10,12)	.	. *
X(3,13)	.	36.00000	X(10,13)	.	. *
X(3,14)	.	36.00000	X(10,14)	9.00000	.
X(3,15)	.	36.00000	X(10,15)	3.00000	.
X(3,16)	.	36.00000	X(10,16)	.	. *
X(3,17)	.	48.00000	X(10,17)	.	12.00000
X(3,18)	.	60.00000	X(10,18)	.	24.00000
X(3,23)	.	84.00000	X(10,23)	.	48.00000
X(3,24)	.	84.00000	X(10,24)	.	48.00000
X(3,25)	.	88.00000	X(10,25)	.	52.00000
X(3,26)	.	94.00000	X(10,26)	.	58.00000
X(3,D)	.	6.00000	X(10,D)	.	12.00000
X(7,4)	.	12.00000	X(11,4)	.	48.00000
X(7,5)	2.00000	.	X(11,5)	.	36.00000
X(7,6)	6.00000	.	X(11,6)	.	36.00000

NAME	ACTIVITY	REDUCED COST		NAME	ACTIVITY	REDUCED COST	
X(7,12)	.	12.00000		X(11,12)	.	.	*
X(7,13)	.	12.00000		X(11,13)	8.00000	.	
X(7,14)	.	12.00000		X(11,14)	.	.	*
X(7,15)	.	12.00000		X(11,15)	.	.	*
X(7,16)	.	12.00000		X(11,16)	.	.	*
X(7,17)	.	24.00000		X(11,17)	.	12.00000	
X(7,18)	.	36.00000		X(11,18)	.	24.00000	
X(7,23)	.	60.00000		X(11,23)	.	48.00000	
X(7,24)	.	60.00000		X(11,24)	.	48.00000	
X(7,25)	.	64.00000		X(11,25)	.	52.00000	
X(7,26)	.	10.00000		X(11,26)	.	58.00000	
X(7,D)	.	6.00000		X(11,D)	.	18.00000	
X(19,4)	.	108.00000		X(22,4)	.	132.00000	
X(19,5)	.	96.00000		X(22,5)	.	120.00000	
X(19,6)	.	96.00000		X(22,6)	.	120.00000	
X(19,12)	.	48.00000		X(22,12)	.	72.00000	
X(19,13)	.	36.00000		X(22,13)	.	60.00000	
X(19,14)	.	24.00000		X(22,14)	.	48.00000	
X(19,15)	.	12.00000		X(22,15)	.	36.00000	
X(19,16)	4.00000	.		X(22,16)	.	24.00000	
X(19,17)	4.00000	.		X(22,17)	.	24.00000	
X(19,18)	.	.	*	X(22,18)	.	24.00000	
X(19,23)	.	12.00000		X(22,23)	.	.	*
X(19,24)	.	12.00000		X(22,24)	2.00000	.	
X(19,25)	.	16.00000		X(22,25)	.	4.00000	
X(19,26)	.	22.00000		X(22,26)	.	10.00000	
X(19,D)	.	30.00000		X(22,D)	.	36.00000	
X(20,4)	.	108.00000		X(B,4)	.	38.00000	
X(20,5)	.	96.00000		X(B,5)	.	32.00000	
X(20,6)	.	96.00000		X(B,6)	.	38.00000	
X(20,12)	.	48.00000		X(B,12)	.	26.00000	
X(20,13)	.	36.00000		X(B,13)	.	20.00000	
X(20,14)	.	24.00000		X(B,14)	.	14.00000	
X(20,15)	.	12.00000		X(B,15)	.	8.00000	
X(20,16)	.	.	*	X(B,16)	.	2.00000	
X(20,17)	4.00000	.		X(B,17)	.	8.00000	
X(20,18)	6.00000	.		X(B,18)	.	14.00000	
X(20,23)	2.00000	.		X(B,23)	.	8.00000	
X(20,24)	.	.	*	X(B,24)	.	2.00000	
X(20,25)	.	4.00000		X(B,25)	3.00000	.	
X(20,26)	.	10.00000		X(B,26)	2.00000	.	
X(20,D)	.	24.00000					
X(21,4)	.	120.00000					
X(21,5)	.	108.00000					
X(21,6)	.	108.00000					
X(21,12)	.	60.00000					
X(21,13)	.	48.00000					
X(21,14)	.	36.00000					
X(21,15)	.	24.00000					
X(21,16)	.	12.00000					
X(21,17)	.	12.00000					
X(21,18)	.	12.00000					
X(21,23)	2.00000	.					
X(21,24)	4.00000	.					
X(21,25)	.	4.00000					
X(21,26)	.	10.00000					
X(21,D)	.	30.00000					

Display 4.2. Portion of computer output for the contractor's decision with borrow and disposal opportunities.

excavation, haul (between section i and section j), and placement. Similar unit costs, $C(i,D)$ and $C(B,j)$, are calculated for moving material to disposal sites and from borrow pits, respectively.

Objective. The objective, typically, is to minimize the total cost of earthmoving. Total cost is the sum of costs of moving earth from section to section, from the borrow pit(s) to sections of fill, and from sections of cut to the disposal site(s). In symbols, the total cost of earthmoving Z is:

$$Z = \sum_i \sum_j C(i,j)X(i,j) + \sum_j C(B,j)X(B,j) + \sum_i C(i,D)X(i,D)$$

where the double summation $(\sum_i \sum_j)$ represents a short-hand notation for adding the products $C(i,j)X(i,j)$ for every pair of values of i and j.

Constraints. Naturally, the values of the decision variables are limited by such factors as the required quantities of cut and fill and the capacities of the disposal and borrow sites.

In symbols, constraints on the quantity of cut are written as:

$$X(i,1) + X(i,2) + \cdots + X(i,D) = Q_c(i)$$

where the left-hand side is the sum of material to be moved from section i to each section of fill and each disposal site, and $Q_c(i)$ is the cut required in section i. A constraint is included for each section of cut.

Similarly, for fill:

$$X(1,j) + X(2,j) + \cdots + X(B,j) = Q_f(j)$$

where the left-hand side is the sum of material taken from each section of cut and borrow to provide the required fill $Q_f(j)$ in section j. Again, a constraint of this type is included for each section requiring fill.

Capacity considerations of borrow and disposal sites can be included by using constraints such as:

$$X(B,1) + X(B,2) + \cdots + X(B,n) \leq Q_B$$

and

$$X(1,D) + X(2,D) + \cdots + X(n,D) \leq Q_D$$

where Q_B and Q_D are the total borrow available and the capacity of the disposal site, respectively, and n is the total number of roadway sections.

The Optimal Solution. The nonnegative values of the various X's that minimize the equation for Z, consistent with the constraints, can be determined routinely by computer using a linear programming routine. Often, alternative optimal solutions exist. These can be obtained and compared to select the more satisfactory one.

CHAPTER 5

MORE ON MINIMIZING EARTHMOVING COSTS

The last chapter developed a modern method based upon linear programming for planning the logistics of an earthmoving operation. Not only does this method provide information similar to that obtained by the conventional mass diagram method, it can also be adapted skillfully to situations for which mass diagram methods are unsuitable. These include practical situations in which haul costs and soil properties vary along the roadway, and when borrow sites or landfills may be developed to reduce earthmoving costs. This chapter shows how to deal with these situations. Readers may find it helpful to review the final section of Chapter 4.

5.1 VARIATION IN HAUL COSTS

Figure 5.1 shows plan and profile views of a proposed roadway and the estimates of cut and fill quantities. A borrow pit of 100,000-cubic-yard capacity is located near station 5, and a landfill of 300,000-cubic-yard capacity is located near the beginning of the roadway (station 0).

Table 5.1 summarizes the components of earthmoving costs, that is, the costs of excavation, haul, and placement. Sections 3 and 6 include haul costs for moving soil within them because both cut and fill are involved. Note that haul costs are not directly proportional to distance. For example, the cost of moving 1000 cubic yards of soil from section 2 to section 3 is $400, while the cost from section 3 to section 4 (an equal distance) is $450. Likewise, the haul cost per thousand cubic yards from section 3 to section 6 is $900, but from section 6 to section 3 it is $1100, and so on. These variations arise from the particular topography.

Again, the problem is to determine how much earth should be moved and from where to where to minimize total cost. Using the data in Table 5.1, an objective equation that takes account of the varying haul

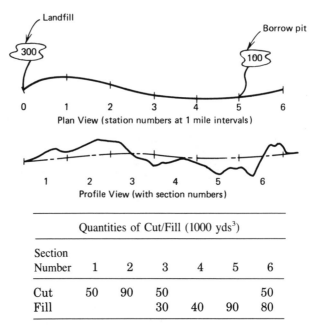

Quantities of Cut/Fill (1000 yds³)

Section Number	1	2	3	4	5	6
Cut	50	90	50			50
Fill			30	40	90	80

Figure 5.1. Plan and profile views of proposed roadway with estimated quantities of cut and fill.

TABLE 5.1.   Cost Data.*

Excavation (including loading):
  along roadway $ 800
  from borrow pit $ 550
Placement (including compaction):
  along roadway $1800
  at landfill $ 350
Haul:

Sections of Cut	Sections of Fill				
	3	4	5	6	D
1	700	950	1200	1400	400
2	400	650	900	1100	650
3	200	450	700	900	950
6	1100	800	450	200	1650
B	1050	750	400	300	—

*All entries in dollars per thousand cubic yards.

costs (as well as the costs of excavation and placement) is:

minimize:

$$Z = 3300X(1,3) + 3550X(1,4) + 3800X(1,5) + 4000X(1,6)$$
$$+ 1550X(1,D) + 3000X(2,3) + 3250X(2,4) + 3500X(2,5)$$
$$+ 3700X(2,6) + 1800X(2,D) + 2800X(3,3) + 3050X(3,4)$$
$$+ 3300X(3,5) + 3500X(3,6) + 2100X(3,D) + 3700X(6,3)$$
$$+ 3400X(6,4) + 3050X(6,5) + 2800X(6,6) + 2800X(6,D)$$
$$+ 3400X(B,3) + 3100X(B,4) + 2750X(B,5) + 2650X(B,6)$$

where, as earlier, $X(1,3)$ is a variable representing the amount of material (in thousands of cubic yards) to be moved from section 1 to section 3, and so on. The coefficients are, of course, the unit costs of earthmoving. For example, the cost to move 1000 cubic yards of soil from section 1 to section 3 is the sum of the unit costs of excavation, haul, and placement, that is, \$800 + \$700 + \$1800 = \$3300. The coefficient of $X(B,3)$ is determined by \$550 + \$1050 + \$1800 = \$3400. The remaining coefficients are obtained similarly.

The constraint for cut in section 1 can be expressed as:

$$X(1,3) + X(1,4) + X(1,5) + X(1,6) + X(1,D) = 50$$

since 50,000 cubic yards of cut are required. For sections 2, 3, and 6, the cut constraints are:

$$X(2,3) + X(2,4) + X(2,5) + X(2,6) + X(2,D) = 90$$
$$X(3,3) + X(3,4) + X(3,5) + X(3,6) + X(3,D) = 50$$
$$X(6,3) + X(6,4) + X(6,5) + X(6,6) + X(6,D) = 50$$

The constraint equation

$$X(1,3) + X(2,3) + X(3,3) + X(6,3) + X(B,3) = 30$$

expresses the fill required in section 3. For sections 4, 5, and 6, the fill constraints are:

$$X(1,4) + X(2,4) + X(3,4) + X(6,4) + X(B,4) = 40$$
$$X(1,5) + X(2,5) + X(3,5) + X(6,5) + X(B,5) = 90$$
$$X(1,6) + X(2,6) + X(3,6) + X(6,6) + X(B,6) = 80$$

Finally, the capacity limitations at the borrow pit and the landfill are written, respectively, as:

$$X(B,3) + X(B,4) + X(B,5) + X(B,6) \leq 100$$

and

$$X(1,D) + X(2,D) + X(3,D) + X(6,D) \leq 300$$

The objective equation and the constraints, together with the obvious requirement that none of the variables have negative values, form a linear programming problem. The complete formulation appears in Display 5.1. The solution shows $Z^* = \$791,000$, while the sensitivity analysis indicates that there are multiple solutions. Recall from the discussion regarding Display 4.1 that if a variable "will enter the solution if its cost is decreased," it will have a positive value in at least one other solution (yielding the same value of Z^*). Therefore, variables $X(1,6)$ and $X(2,4)$, among others, will be positive in alternative solutions. Some of the multiple solutions, obtained through additional computer-aided computation, are shown in Figure 5.2.

Neither the borrow pit nor the landfill are indicated in any of the multiple solutions, even though they appear economical. For example, the unit costs of borrow for filling sections 5 and 6 are significantly less than those using material from any section of cut, that is, section 1, 2, 3, or 6.

```
#
RUN $DELIBR/LP
#RUNNING 4335
TYPE HELP IF YOU NEED IT
--> #?
LOAD
ENTER OBJECTIVE FUNCTION:
OBJ*FN: MIN   3300 X13 + 3550 X14 + 3800 X15 + 4000 X16 + 1550 X1D +,
              3000 X23 + 3250 X24 + 3500 X25 + 3700 X26 + 1800 X2D +,
              2800 X33 + 3050 X34 + 3300 X35 + 3500 X36 + 2100 X3D +,
              3700 X63 + 3400 X64 + 3050 X65 + 2800 X66 + 2800 X6D +,
              3400 XB3 + 3100 XB4 + 2750 XB5 + 2650 XB6
ENTER CONSTRAINTS:
CON1:           X13 + X14 + X15 + X16 + X1D = 50
CON2:           X23 + X24 + X25 + X26 + X2D = 90
CON3:           X33 + X34 + X35 + X36 + X3D = 50
CON4:           X63 + X64 + X65 + X66 + X6D = 50
CON5:           X13 + X23 + X33 + X63 + XB3 = 30
CON6:           X14 + X24 + X34 + X64 + XB4 = 40
CON7:           X15 + X25 + X35 + X65 + XB5 = 90
CON8:           X16 + X26 + X36 + X66 + XB6 = 80
CON9:           XB3 + XB4 + XB5 + XB6      <=100
CON10:          X1D + X2D + X3D + X6D      <=300
CON11:
-->   NONE
-->   SENSITIVITY
-->   SOLVE

OBJECTIVE FUNCTION ATTAINS A MINIMUM VALUE OF 791000 AT:
                X23 =      20.00
                X35 =      50.00
                X66 =      50.00
                X13 =      10.00
                X14 =      40.00
                X25 =      40.00
                X26 =      30.00

ALL OTHER VARIABLES HAVE A VALUE OF ZERO.
```

57

SENSITIVITY ANALYSIS:

 X16 WILL ENTER THE SOLUTION IF ITS COST IS DECREASED. CURRENTLY
THIS IS SET AT 4000.

 XB6 WILL ENTER THE SOLUTION IF ITS COST IS DECREASED TO 2450.
CURRENTLY THIS IS SET AT 2650.

 X2D WILL ENTER THE SOLUTION IF ITS COST IS DECREASED TO 1250.
CURRENTLY THIS IS SET AT 1800.

 X24 WILL ENTER THE SOLUTION IF ITS COST IS DECREASED. CURRENTLY
THIS IS SET AT 3250.

 X33 WILL ENTER THE SOLUTION IF ITS COST IS DECREASED. CURRENTLY
THIS IS SET AT 2800.

 X34 WILL ENTER THE SOLUTION IF ITS COST IS DECREASED. CURRENTLY
THIS IS SET AT 3050.

 X36 WILL ENTER THE SOLUTION IF ITS COST IS DECREASED. CURRENTLY
THIS IS SET AT 3500.

 X3D WILL ENTER THE SOLUTION IF ITS COST IS DECREASED TO 1050.
CURRENTLY THIS IS SET AT 2100.

 X63 WILL ENTER THE SOLUTION IF ITS COST IS DECREASED TO 2100.
CURRENTLY THIS IS SET AT 3700.

 X64 WILL ENTER THE SOLUTION IF ITS COST IS DECREASED TO 2350.
CURRENTLY THIS IS SET AT 3400.

 X65 WILL ENTER THE SOLUTION IF ITS COST IS DECREASED TO 2600.
CURRENTLY THIS IS SET AT 3050.

 X6D WILL ENTER THE SOLUTION IF ITS COST IS DECREASED TO 350.
CURRENTLY THIS IS SET AT 2800.

 XB3 WILL ENTER THE SOLUTION IF ITS COST IS DECREASED TO 1750.
CURRENTLY THIS IS SET AT 3400.

 XB4 WILL ENTER THE SOLUTION IF ITS COST IS DECREASED TO 2000.
CURRENTLY THIS IS SET AT 3100.

 XB5 WILL ENTER THE SOLUTION IF ITS COST IS DECREASED TO 2250.
CURRENTLY THIS IS SET AT 2750.

 X15 WILL ENTER THE SOLUTION IF ITS COST IS DECREASED. CURRENTLY
THIS IS SET AT 3800.

 100 UNITS OF THE CON9 SUPPLY REMAIN UNUSED. CURRENTLY THIS IS SET
AT 100.

 300 UNITS OF THE CON10 SUPPLY REMAIN UNUSED. CURRENTLY THIS IS SET
AT 300.

--> STOP

Display 5.1. Linear programming formulation and solution for the problem of varying
haul costs.

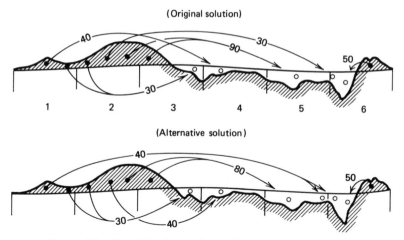

Figure 5.2. Pictorial solution for problem of varying haul costs.

However, note that the total quantities of cut and fill along the roadway are exactly equal. Therefore, if borrow material is used as fill, an equal quantity of cut would have to be excavated and disposed of elsewhere (in this case, at the landfill) at an additional cost. The advantage of the borrow pit is eroded by the added costs of disposal.

The sensitivity analysis shows that, other costs being equal, borrow would be economical in section 6 if its unit cost was reduced by $200, that is, to $2450 per thousand cubic yards. Similarly, it would be economical in section 5 if its unit cost were as low as $2250 per thousand cubic yards, and so on. The computational cost for this example, including the sensitivity analysis, was 23¢ on the Burroughs B7700 computer.

5.2. SWELL AND SHRINKAGE FACTORS

Earth volumes typically increase as a consequence of excavation and are decreased by compaction. The extent depends upon such factors as the type of soil, in situ conditions, and the modes of excavation, handling, and compaction. Engineers use *swell factors* and *shrinkage factors* to represent the percentage volume changes from in situ conditions. In practice, soil conditions vary from site to site, and allowance made for swell and shrinkage when considering the logistics of earthmoving.

The previous section demonstrated that the usual complexities of accounting for variable haul costs are sidestepped by the linear programming method. Much the same is true when dealing with swell and shrinkage factors.

Continuing the previous example, suppose that the volume of roadway cut expands by 50% when excavated (that is, its swell factor is 1.5). This means that each 1000 cubic yards of in situ roadway soil (cut) becomes 1500 cubic yards upon excavation. The latter figure is the relevant one for haul and compaction purposes. For the borrow pit, assume that the swell factor is 1.1, and suppose that the contract specifications require that all soils (both borrow and cut) be compacted to 95% of their original in situ volumes (that is, the shrinkage factor is 0.95). This means that 1000 cubic yards of cut or borrow will provide only 950 cubic yards of fill.

In practice, the component unit costs of earthmoving will vary with the soils and methods used. However, for simplicity, assume that the cost data shown in Table 5.1 remain unchanged. The unit cost coefficients of the earlier objective function must be recalculated to account for the swell factor. For example, the cost of moving 1000 cubic yards of soil from section 1 to section 3 is obtained by adding $800 for excavation, $700 × 1.5 = $1050 for haul, and $1800 × 1.5 = $2700 for placement, for a total of $4550 (rather than the $3550 obtained earlier). The factor 1.5 is, of course, the swell factor for cut. Since the swell factor for borrow is 1.1, moving 1000 cubic yards of borrow to section 3 will cost $550 + $1155 (= $1050 × 1.1) + $1980 (= $1800 × 1.1), for a total of $3685. The remaining coefficients are calculated similarly. The revised objective equation is:

minimize:

$$
\begin{aligned}
Z = {} & 4550X(1,3) + 4925X(1,4) + 5300X(1,5) + 5600X(1,6) + 1925X(1,D) \\
& + 4100X(2,3) + 4475X(2,4) + 4850X(2,5) + 5150X(2,6) + 2300X(2,D) \\
& + 3800X(3,3) + 4175X(3,4) + 4550X(3,5) + 4850X(3,6) + 2750X(3,D) \\
& + 5150X(6,3) + 4700X(6,4) + 4175X(6,5) + 3800X(6,6) + 3800X(6,D) \\
& + 3685X(B,3) + 3355X(B,4) + 2970X(B,5) + 2860X(B,6)
\end{aligned}
$$

The four cut constraints and the borrow pit capacity constraint remain unchanged. The reason is that each variable in these constraints refers to an in situ volume, that is, prior to excavation.

The fill constraints for sections 3, 4, 5, and 6 require modification to account for the required compaction (shrinkage). Each $X(i,j)$ in these constraints is multiplied by 0.95, since 1 cubic yard of material becomes 0.95 cubic yard after compaction. The revised fill constraints are:

$$0.95X(1,3) + 0.95X(2,3) + 0.95X(3,3) + 0.95X(6,3) + 0.95X(B,3) = 30$$

$$0.95X(1,4) + 0.95X(2,4) + 0.95X(3,4) + 0.95X(6,4) + 0.95X(B,4) = 40$$

$$0.95X(1,5) + 0.95X(2,5) + 0.95X(3,5) + 0.95X(6,5) + 0.95X(B,5) = 90$$

$$0.95X(1,6) + 0.95X(2,6) + 0.95X(3,6) + 0.95X(6,6) + 0.95X(B,6) = 80$$

Finally, since compaction is not required at the landfill, the "expanded" soil deposited there will occupy a 50% greater volume than before

```
#
RUN $DELIBR/LP
#RUNNING 4529
TYPE HELP IF YOU NEED IT
-->  #?
LOAD
ENTER OBJECTIVE FUNCTION:
OBJ*FN: MIN  4550 X13 + 4925 X14 + 5300 X15 + 5600 X16 + 1925 X1D +,
             4100 X23 + 4475 X24 + 4850 X25 + 5150 X26 + 2300 X2D +,
             3800 X33 + 4175 X34 + 4550 X35 + 4850 X36 + 2750 X3D +,
             5150 X63 + 4700 X64 + 4175 X65 + 3800 X66 + 3800 X6D +,
             3685 XB3 + 3355 XB4 + 2970 XB5 + 2860 XB6
ENTER CONSTRAINTS:
CON1:            X13 +       X14 +       X15 +       X16 +       X1D = 50
CON2:            X23 +       X24 +       X25 +       X26 +       X2D = 90
CON3:            X33 +       X34 +       X35 +       X36 +       X3D = 50
CON4:            X63 +       X64 +       X65 +       X66 +       X6D = 50
CON5:      0.95 X13 + 0.95 X23 + 0.95 X33 + 0.95 X63 + 0.95 XB3 = 30
CON6:      0.95 X14 + 0.95 X24 + 0.95 X34 + 0.95 X64 + 0.95 XB4 = 40
CON7:      0.95 X15 + 0.95 X25 + 0.95 X35 + 0.95 X65 + 0.95 XB5 = 90
CON8:      0.95 X16 + 0.95 X26 + 0.95 X36 + 0.95 X66 + 0.95 XB6 = 80
CON9:            XB3 +       XB4 +       XB5 +       XB6            <=100
CON10:     1.5 X1D +   1.5 X2D +  1.5 X3D +  1.5 X6D              <=300
CON11:


-->  NONE
-->  SOLVE


OBJECTIVE FUNCTION ATTAINS A MINIMUM VALUE OF 1093028.947 AT:
                     X1D =        50.00
                     XB6 =        34.21
                     XB5 =        28.42
                     X66 =        50.00
                     X23 =        31.58
                     X34 =        42.11
                     X25 =        58.42
                     X35 =         7.89

        ALL OTHER VARIABLES HAVE A VALUE OF ZERO.

-->  STOP
```

Display 5.2. Linear programming formulation and solution with swell and shrinkage.

excavation. This affects the capacity constraint for the landfill, which becomes:

$$1.5X(1,D) + 1.5X(2,D) + 1.5X(3,D) + 1.5X(6,D) \leq 300$$

Once again, the (revised) objective equation and the constraints, with the nonnegativity condition, represent a linear programming problem. The solution appears in Display 5.2. The minimum total earthmoving cost has increased to $1,093,029. This increase from the earlier $791,000 is due to the increased volumes hauled and placed because of soil expansion.

In the previous example, the required quantities of cut and fill were equally matched. Here, however, some borrow was needed to make up the

5% volume loss from compaction. Yet, the optimal solution utilizes both the borrow pit and the landfill, that is:

$$X(B,5) = 28.42, \qquad X(B,6) = 34.21, \qquad X(1,D) = 50$$

If this 50,000 cubic yards of soil from section 1 were used as fill in sections 5 and 6, it would save \$17,500 (= 50,000 cubic yards × \$350 per thousand) in disposal costs and another \$27,500 (= 50,000 cubic yards × \$550 per thousand) in borrow excavation costs. However, the haul distances from section 1 to sections 5 and 6 are farther and more costly than those from the borrow pit. Also, because of the difference in swell factors, a greater quantity of roadway material, after expansion, would have to be hauled and compacted to satisfy the same volume of fill. Therefore, as the linear programming solution shows, the additional disposal costs and excavation costs associated with using the landfill and borrow pit are more than offset by the savings in haul and compaction.

5.3. SETUP COSTS

The availability of a borrow pit and a landfill contributed to minimizing total earthmoving costs in the preceding example. Their locations were assumed to be fixed. However, sometimes there is a choice in the number and the location of borrow and disposal sites, any of which may further reduce costs. When there is such flexibility, questions arise as to how many borrow and disposal sites should be established and where they should be located.

Deciding whether to set up borrow and disposal sites usually depends upon such associated costs as:

1. Land acquisition (or right-of-way).
2. Site preparation for excavation or for dumping.
3. Construction and maintenance of access roads.
4. Refurbishing and cleanup.

A little skill and imagination extends the linear programming method to deal with these added questions of how many? and where?

Suppose that there is a proposal to establish a borrow site along the access road to the borrow pit of the previous example (see Figure 5.3). The setup cost for such a site is estimated to be \$10,000, and the excavation and placement costs are estimated as \$700 and \$1800, respectively, per thousand cubic yards. The possible advantage of this additional site is the economy in certain of the hauling costs which are estimated as \$800, \$500, \$150, and \$150 per thousand cubic yards to the respective sections 3, 4, 5, and 6. The soil is anticipated to have the same swell factor

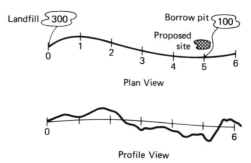

Figure 5.3. Roadway plan and profile views with proposed borrow site.

as the borrow pit (that is, 1.1) and to require compaction to 95% of its original volume. There is a capacity limitation of 40,000 cubic yards at the proposed site, as additional excavation might undermine the roadway's slope stability.

How can the earlier example be modified to include the economies of an additional borrow site?

First, new variables are needed, say $X(S, 3)$, $X(S, 4)$, $X(S, 5)$, and $X(S, 6)$, to represent the thousands of cubic yards of borrow to be hauled from the proposed site to sections 3, 4, 5, and 6, respectively. The earth-moving costs involved with the site include the $10,000 setup cost plus the combined costs of excavation, haul, and compaction for each of the four sections of fill. The unit cost coefficients for the four new variables are determined as in the previous example and are equal to $3560, $3230, $2845, and $2845, respectively, per thousand cubic yards. Therefore, if the borrow pit is established, the terms:

$$\$10{,}000 + 3560X(S, 3) + 3230X(S, 4) + 2845X(S, 5) + 2845(S, 6)$$

should be added to the objective equation of the previous example. How-ever, if the proposed borrow site is not utilized, none of these terms should appear in the objective equation. Here is a dilemma. To obtain the optimal solution to a linear programming problem, a definite objective equation is required; yet, one cannot be written until an optimal solution is available to indicate whether or not the proposed borrow site should be utilized.

In simple cases (as this one), two linear programming problems could be formulated: one neglecting the borrow site and the other including it. A comparison of the two solutions would indicate whether the proposed site is economical. However, this procedure is unwieldy when the number of possible combinations of sites is large. Fortunately, all borrow and disposal sites can be considered in one linear programming formulation using a clever mathematical trick.

Introduce a new variable Y which can equal 0 or 1, but nothing else. It should take the value zero if the proposed borrow site is not utilized, and unity otherwise. In symbols,

$$Y = 0 \quad \text{when } X(S, 3) + X(S, 4) + X(S, 5) + X(S, 6) = 0$$

and

$$Y = 1 \quad \text{when } X(S,3) + X(S,4) + X(S,5) + X(S,6) > 0$$

The expression:

$$\$10{,}000Y + 3560X(S,3) + 3230X(S,4) + 2845X(S,5) + 2845X(S,6)$$

is the same as the earlier expression, except that $10,000 is now multiplied by Y. This is precisely what was needed. Now, when the new site is utilized, $Y = 1$, and the setup cost is included. When it is not, the $10,000 is eliminated because it is multiplied by $Y = 0$.

So far we have only indicated how we want Y to behave. Several constraints are used to ensure the desired behavior. First, the constraint

$$Y \leq 1$$

ensures that Y does not exceed unity. Of course, as for all other variables in the problem, Y will not be negative. Next, the constraint

$$X(S,3) + X(S,4) + X(S,5) + X(S,6) \leq 40Y$$

ensures that Y will be greater than zero whenever any of the $X(S,j)$ values are positive. Of course, if all the $X(S,j)$ are zero, the linear programming solution will choose $Y = 0$ to eliminate the setup cost. Finally, Y is required to be an integer.

The coefficient for the right-hand side of the last constraint was chosen with some foresight. Actually, any coefficient would be satisfactory provided it is large enough (in this case, greater than or equal to 40) that it does not interfere with a capacity constraint for the borrow site. By using a coefficient equal to 40, this constraint also serves as the capacity constraint.

Each of the four fill constraints of the previous example must be modified to reflect the possible use of borrow site material. Specifically, the terms $0.95X(S,3)$, $0.95X(S,4)$, $0.95X(S,5)$, and $0.95X(S,6)$ are added to the left-hand sides of the four constraints. The four cut constraints and the capacity constraints for the borrow pit and the landfill remain unchanged since they are unaffected by the proposed borrow site.

This completes the modifications for considering the borrow site. The complete formulation is shown in Display 5.3.

The minimum cost of $1,093,029 is the same as in Display 5.2. The reason is clear since the variable Y [and each $(X(S,j)$] is zero, indicating that the proposed borrow site is not used. Some of the variables, notably $X(2,4)$, $X(2,5)$, $X(3,4)$, and $X(3,5)$, have different values than in the earlier solution. This simply means that an alternate solution yielding the same minimum cost has been identified. The reduced costs of variables $X(3,3)$ and $X(3,4)$ are both zero. As indicated in Chapter 4, one (or more) of the multiple solutions must call for using the cut in section 3

FORMULATION:

```
MINIMIZE Z =   4550X13 + 4925X14 + 5300X15 + 5600X16 + 1925X1D
             + 4100X23 + 4475X24 + 4850X25 + 5150X26 + 2300X2D
             + 3800X33 + 4175X34 + 4550X35 + 4850X36 + 2750X3D
             + 5150X63 + 4700X64 + 4175X65 + 3800X66 + 3800X6D
             + 3685XB3 + 3355XB4 + 2970XB5 + 2860XB6 + 10000Y
             + 3560XS3 + 3230XS4 + 2845XS5 + 2845XS6
CUT1:          X13 + X14 + X15 + X16 + X1D =  50
CUT2:          X23 + X24 + X25 + X26 + X2D =  90
CUT3:          X33 + X34 + X35 + X36 + X3D =  50
CUT6:          X63 + X64 + X65 + X66 + X6D =  50
FILL3:         0.95X13 + 0.95X23 + 0.95X33 + 0.95X63 + 0.95XB3
             + 0.95XS3 =  30
FILL4:         0.95X14 + 0.95X24 + 0.95X34 + 0.95X64 + 0.95XB4
             + 0.95XS4 =  40
FILL5:         0.95X15 + 0.95X25 + 0.95X35 + 0.95X65 + 0.95XB5
             + 0.95XS5 =  90
FILL6:         0.95X16 + 0.95X26 + 0.95X36 + 0.95X66 + 0.95XB6
             + 0.95XS6 =  80
BPC :          XB3 + XB4 + XB5 + XB6 <= 100
LFC :          1.5X1D + 1.5X2D + 1.5X3D + 1.5X6D <= 300
INTY:          Y <= 1
BSC :          XS3 + XS4 + XS5 + XS6 - 40Y <= 0
```

AND   X13, X14, ..., XB6 , XS3 , ..., XS6 ≥ 0; Y ≥ 0 AND INTEGER.

SOLUTION:	NAME	ACTIVITY	INPUT COST	REDUCED COST	
	Z	1093028.94737		.	
	X13		4550.00000	405.00000	
	X14	.	4925.00000	405.00000	
	X15	.	5300.00000	405.00000	
	X16	.	5600.00000	815.00000	
	X1D	50.00000	1925.00000	.	
	X23	31.57895	4100.00000	.	
	X24	42.10526	4475.00000	.	
	X25	16.31579	4850.00000	.	
	X26	.	5150.00000	410.00000	
	X2D	.	2300.00000	420.00000	
	X33	.	3800.00000	.	*
	X34	.	4175.00000	.	*
	X35	50.00000	4550.00000	.	
	X36	.	4850.00000	410.00000	
	X3D	.	2750.00000	1170.00000	
	X63	.	5150.00000	1990.00000	
	X64	.	4700.00000	1165.00000	
	X65	.	4175.00000	265.00000	
	X66	50.00000	3800.00000	.	
	X6D	.	3800.00000	2860.00000	
	XB3	.	3685.00000	1465.00000	
	XB4	.	3355.00000	760.00000	
	XB5	28.42105	2970.00000	.	
	XB6	34.21053	2860.00000	.	
	Y	.	10000.00000	.	
	XS3	.	3560.00000	1590.00000	
	XS4	.	3230.00000	885.00000	
	XS5	.	2845.00000	125.00000	
	XS6	.	2845.00000	235.00000	

Display 5.3. Linear programming formulation and solution for minimizing earthmoving costs with a $10,000 setup cost for borrow pit.

FORMULATION:

```
MINIMIZE Z = 4550X13 + 4925X14 + 5300X15 + 5600X16 + 1925X1D
             + 4100X23 + 4475X24 + 4850X25 + 5150X26 + 2300X2D
             + 3800X33 + 4175X34 + 4550X35 + 4850X36 + 2750X3D
             + 5150X63 + 4700X64 + 4175X65 + 3800X66 + 3800X6D
             + 3685XB3 + 3355XB4 + 2970XB5 + 2860XB6 + 3500Y
             + 3560XS3 + 3230XS4 + 2845XS5 + 2845XS6
```

CUT1:	X13 + X14 + X15 + X16 + X1D = 50
CUT2:	X23 + X24 + X25 + X26 + X2D = 90
CUT3:	X33 + X34 + X35 + X36 + X3D = 50
CUT6:	X63 + X64 + X65 + X66 + X6D = 50
FILL3:	0.95X13 + 0.95X23 + 0.95X33 + 0.95X63 + 0.95XB3
	+ 0.95XS3 = 30
FILL4:	0.95X14 + 0.95X24 + 0.95X34 + 0.95X64 + 0.95XB4
	+ 0.95XS4 = 40
FILL5:	0.95X15 + 0.95X25 + 0.95X35 + 0.95X65 + 0.95XB5
	+ 0.95XS5 = 90
FILL6:	0.95X16 + 0.95X26 + 0.95X36 + 0.95X66 + 0.95XB6
	+ 0.95XS6 = 80
BPC :	XB3 + XB4 + XB5 + XB6 <= 100
LFC :	1.5X1D + 1.5X2D + 1.5X3D + 1.5X6D <= 300
INTY:	Y <= 1
BSC :	XS3 + XS4 + XS5 + XS6 - 40Y <= 0

AND   X13, X14, ..., XB6, XS3, ..., XS6 $\geq$ 0; Y $\geq$ 0 AND INTEGER.

SOLUTION:

COST, Z = 1092802.63187

X1D = 50.00000	X66 = 50.00000
X23 = 31.57895	XB6 = 22.63158
X24 = 42.10526	XS5 = 28.42105
X25 = 16.31579	XS6 = 11.57895
X35 = 50.00000	and, Y = 1.0

Display 5.4. Linear programming formulation and solution for minimizing earthmoving costs with a $3500 setup cost for borrow pit.

as fill in sections 3 and/or 4. The previous discussions on identifying and choosing among multiple solutions apply here as well.

The proposed borrow site was not practical for a setup cost of $10,000. What if its setup cost were only $3500? Display 5.4 shows the revised formulation and solution. Here only the coefficient of the variable Y has been changed (to $3500). In this solution, $Z^* = \$1,092,803$ and all 40,000 cubic yards of site material are used as fill in sections 5 and 6 (instead of borrow pit material). The lesser total cost reflects the advantage of establishing the borrow pit (for only $3500).

For simplicity, this example considered establishing only one borrow site, at a specific location. If several borrow sites are possible, the preceding modifications are repeated for each candidate site. Of course, distinct zero–one variables such as $Y1$, $Y2$, and so on, should be used for each site. If additional disposal sites are contemplated, the modifications would be similar, except that the cut constraints (and not the fill constraints) would be altered. Properly formulated, the linear programming solution will indicate which sites should be established and the intensity with which each should be used.

5.4. SUMMARY

This chapter has extended the earthwork distribution problem of the previous chapter to situations involving variable haul costs and soil characteristics, and the establishment of borrow and disposal sites. The examples were simplified to facilitate discussion and illustration. It should not be difficult to extend the formulation techniques to more extensive and practical situations.

CHAPTER 6

PROJECT SELECTION AND COMPETITIVE BIDDING

Stack & Bricks, masonry subcontractors, seek more work. Four jobs are available: three large office building complexes and a 20-house development. If the housing project is chosen, the prime contractor must be given advance notice of the number of homes Stack & Bricks can complete during the summer months (June–August). The remainder will likely be offered to another subcontractor.

Stack & Bricks estimate the profit from each job as:

Office 1	$20,000
Office 2	25,000
Office 3	32,000
Housing	1,500 per house

Since all four projects seem profitable, they would like to undertake them all. However, the projects are scheduled to begin simultaneously, and Stack & Bricks lack sufficient resources.

Each of the four jobs will require a supervisor. However, Stack & Bricks have only three seasoned supervisors available. Each of the three office projects requires a large hoist, and only two are available. The June–August work-force requirements of each job are:

	Man-Hours Required	
	Masons	Laborers
Office 1	3,000	6,000
Office 2	4,000	9,000
Office 3	5,000	12,000
Housing (per house)	400	1,000

Stack & Bricks will have to hire masons and laborers. They estimate that a total of 11,000 mason-hours and 25,000 laborer-hours will be available during the 3-month period. For the other required resources, the quantities are sufficient so that no account of them is needed.

With this information, Stack & Bricks must decide which choice of projects will maximize their total profit and, if the housing project is included, how many houses can be completed.

6.1. PROJECT SELECTION WITH LIMITED RESOURCES

Stack & Bricks could solve their dilemma by enumerating all possible combinations of projects and eliminating the unfeasible ones. For example, since only two hoists are available, at most two of the office complexes can be chosen. The first and second office complexes require a total of 7000 mason-hours and 15,000 laborer-hours. The remainder of mason-hours (4000) and laborer-hours (10,000) would be adequate to complete 10 houses. Three supervisors are available, so this combination of projects is feasible and yields a profit of:

$$\$20,000 + \$25,000 + \$1,500(10) = \$60,000$$

This amount should be compared with that for completing offices 1 and 3 and, possibly, some of the houses; office complex 1 and the entire housing project; and so on.

The enumeration process is obviously taxing, particularly for practical problems having many limited resources and many types of jobs. Fortunately, again, there is a more efficient way.

Suppose Stack & Bricks considered formulating their problem as a linear program. Specifically, let $X_i(i = 1,2,3,4)$ be zero–one variables such that $X_1 = 1$ if office complex 1 is chosen and $X_1 = 0$ if it is not; and so on for X_2 (the second office complex), X_3 (the third office complex), and X_4 (the housing project). Also, let Y be the number of houses undertaken if the housing project is accepted, that is, $Y = 0$ if $X_4 = 0$, and $Y = 1,2,\ldots,19$ or 20 if $X_4 = 1$.

To maximize their total profit, Stack & Bricks' objective function is:

maximize: $\quad Z = 20X_1 + 25X_2 + 32X_3 + 1.5Y$

in thousands of dollars. The first three terms of the summation represent the profit from the office complexes and the last term is the profit from the housing project, since its profit is proportional to the number of houses Y. Using the data on man-hour requirements, resource constraints for masons and laborers are written:

$$3000X_1 + 4000X_2 + 5000X_3 + 400Y \leq 11,000$$

and

$$6000X_1 + 9000X_2 + 12{,}000X_3 + 1000Y \le 25{,}000$$

Here, again, the number of mason- and laborer-hours required to support the housing project are proportional to the number of houses Y.

Each project requires a supervisor, and since three are available, a resource constraint for supervisors is:

$$X_1 + X_2 + X_3 + X_4 \le 3$$

Note that X_4 is being used instead of Y because one supervisor can manage construction on all of the houses, that is, no more than one supervisor is required for the housing project.

For the hoists, the resource constraint is:

$$X_1 + X_2 + X_3 \le 2$$

since each office complex requires one of the two hoists available.

Finally, since both Y and X_4 were used in the various constraints to represent the housing project, a constraint is required to ensure their proper behavior. Similar to the behavior constraint formed for the setup cost example of Chapter 5, the constraint

$$Y \le 20X_4$$

or, equivalently,

$$20X_4 - Y \ge 0$$

ensures that Y will be no greater than zero when $X_4 = 0$, that is, when no work is planned on the housing project; and $Y \le 20$ when $X_4 = 1$. Of course, the coefficient of 20 was chosen equal to the maximum value of Y.

With the restrictions that $X_1, X_2, X_3,$ and X_4 be zero–one variables, and Y be a nonnegative integer, the linear program formulation is complete. Display 6.1 shows the solution:

$$X_1 = 0, \qquad X_2 = 1, \qquad X_3 = 1, \qquad X_4 = 1, \qquad Y = 4$$

and

$$Z = \$63{,}000$$

In practice, additional resources can usually be obtained, but at a premium cost. For example, an additional supervisor could be hired, workers could be paid overtime wages, or additional equipment (or material) could be purchased or leased. The linear programming formulation makes it easy to consider these possibilities. Simply, the resource limits of the appropriate constraints can be altered and the linear program solved again. The difference in profit between the two solutions can be compared with the costs of additional resources to see whether the latter are warranted.

```
FORMULATION:

MAXIMIZE Z =  20 X1 + 25 X2 + 32 X3 + 0 X4 + 1.5 Y

SUBJECT TO:
                3 X1 +  4 X2 +  5 X3 +        0.4Y   <= 11  (MASONS)
                6 X1 +  9 X2 + 12 X3 +        1.0Y   <= 25  (LABORERS)
                1 X1 +  1 X2 +  1 X3 + 1 X4          <=  3  (FOREMEN)
                1 X1 +  1 X2 +  1 X3                 <=  2  (HOISTS)
                                       20 X4 - 1 Y   >=  0

                X1                                   <=  1
                          X2                         <=  1
                                   X3                <=  1
                                          X4         <=  1

AND, X₁, X₂, X₃, X₄, AND Y NON-NEGATIVE AND INTEGER.
```

```
SOLUTION:
                         PROFIT, Z = 63.0
                            X1 =  0.0
                            X2 =  1.0
                            X3 =  1.0
                            X4 =  1.0
                            Y  =  4.0
```

Display 6.1. Linear programming formulation and solution for maximizing Stack and Bricks' profit.

If the additional cost is directly proportional to the increase in the resource, a more direct solution is possible. For example, suppose Stack & Bricks can lease additional hoists at $1000 each for the summer construction period. Let H be an integer variable equal to the number of hoists to lease. An objective function which accounts for profit as well as for the additional leasing costs is:

$$\text{maximize:} \quad Z = 20X_1 + 25X_2 + 30X_3 + 1.5Y - 1H$$

The hoist constraint should be modified as:

$$X_1 + X_2 + X_3 \le (2 + H)$$

or, equivalently,

$$X_1 + X_2 + X_3 - H \le 2$$

The term $(2 + H)$ is, of course, the number of hoists available, taking account of leasing possibilities.

The new formulation, with the remaining constraints unchanged, is shown in Display 6.2. The solution has not changed ($Z^* = \$63,000$), because even with the availability of additional hoists, the man-hour availability is insufficient to work more than two of the office complexes. However, if overtime charges for masons and laborers were $5.00 and $2.00 per hour, respectively, Display 6.3 shows a new solution. Here M

FORMULATION:

MAXIMIZE Z = 20 X1 + 25 X2 + 32 X3 + 0 X4 + 1.5 Y - 1 H

SUBJECT TO:

```
        3 X1 +  4 X2 +  5 X3 +            0.4Y          <=. 11 (MASONS)
        6 X1 +  9 X2 + 12 X3 +            1.0Y          <= 25 (LABORERS)
        1 X1 +  1 X2 +  1 X3 + 1 X4                     <=  3 (FOREMEN)
        1 X1 +  1 X2 +  1 X3                    - 1 H   <=  2 (HOISTS)
                                20 X4 - 1 Y             >=  0
        X1                                              <=  1
              X2                                        <=  1
                     X3                                 <=  1
                            X4                          <=  1
```

AND X1, X2, X3, X4, Y AND H NON-NEGATIVE AND INTEGER.

SOLUTION:

PROFIT, Z = 63.0

X1 = 0.0	X4 = 1.0
X2 = 1.0	Y = 4.0
X3 = 1.0	H = 0.0

Display 6.2. Linear programming formulation and solution for maximizing Stack and Bricks' profit with leasing possibilities.

FORMULATION:

MAXIMIZE Z = 20 X1 + 25 X2 + 32 X3 + 0 X4 + 1.5 Y - 1 H - 5 M - 2 L

SUBJECT TO:

```
        3 X1 +  4 X2 +  5 X3 +         0.4Y - 1 M <= 11 (MASONS)
        6 X1 +  9 X2 + 12 X3 +         1.0Y - 1 L <= 25 (LABORERS)
        1 X1 +  1 X2 +  1 X3 + 1 X4               <=  3 (FOREMEN)
        1 X1 +  1 X2 +  1 X3                - 1 H <=  2 (HOISTS)
                                20 X4 - 1 Y       >=  0
        X1                                        <=  1
              X2                                  <=  1
                     X3                           <=  1
                            X4                    <=  1
```

AND M AND L NON-NEGATIVE; X_1, X_2, X_3, X_4, Y AND H NON-NEGATIVE AND INTEGER.

SOLUTION:

PROFIT, Z = 67.0

X1 = 1.0	Y = 0.0
X2 = 1.0	H = 1.0
X3 = 1.0	M = 1.0
X4 = 0.0	L = 2.0

Display 6.3. Linear programming formulation and solution for maximizing Stack and Bricks' profit with leasing and overtime possibilities.

represents the number of overtime hours (in thousands) for masons; and L those for laborers. That is, if overtime is permitted, the most profitable mix of jobs is the three office complexes (and no houses). One additional hoist ($H = 1$), 1000 overtime hours for masons ($M = 1$), and 2000 overtime hours for laborers ($L = 2$) are required, and the profit is $Z^* = \$67,000$. The computational costs for Displays 6.1–6.3 were each less than 50¢ on the Burroughs B7700 computer.

This example assumed that Stack & Bricks were able to select projects as desired. Of course, contractors usually compete for work, and often by competitive bidding. The next section considers a linear programming formulation for project selection in a competitive environment.

6.2. PROJECT SELECTION WITH COMPETITION

The management of Bildenhire Construction Inc. is planning to bid on four promising contracts. They involve an office building, an apartment house, a school, and a small shopping mall.

Bildenhire's estimators figure the office building to cost $10.5 million; the apartment house, $8 million; the school, $5.5 million; and the shopping mall, $3 million. The estimators have also assessed the required resources. Of those that are likely to be in short supply, the office and apartment projects each require two tower cranes, and one is required for the school. Each project also requires a large air compressor and a crawler tractor. However, work can be scheduled so that the school and mall projects share the same tractor.

The equipment manager reports that four tower cranes and three large air compressors are available in house. Also, two crawler tractors will be ready to go by the start of construction on any of the four jobs.

Each project requires Bildenhire to submit a bid bond* with its bid. Taking into account Bildenhire's current financial commitments, the bonding company's price for a bid bond is 0.2% of the bid amount, that is, $2000 per $1 million bid. Also, the bonding company will accept, at most, an $18 million *exposure limit*. In other words, the sum total of Bildenhire's bids can not exceed $18 million.

Bildenhire's management must decide which jobs to bid and for how much. They want to maximize their profit, but realize that without successful bids there can be no profit. If they bid high, their profits will be high, but only if they win; and their chances of winning tend to decrease as their bids increase above those of their competitors.

Bildenhire's approach to the two questions is to begin with a searching appraisal of their competition. Who are the likely competitors, and how

---

*A bid bond is an insurance to protect the project's owner in case of contractor default;— perhaps because the necessary skills are lacking or perhaps a more lucrative opportunity has surfaced.

TABLE 6.1.   Bildenhire's Bid Analysis Data.

Project	Estimated Cost (million $)	Bid (million $)	Chance of Winning	C-W-P (million $)	
1. Office	10.5	11.0	0.60	0.30	
building		11.5	0.40	0.40	*
		12.0	0.20	0.30	
		12.5	0.10	0.20	
2. Apartment	8.0	8.5	0.50	0.25	
		9.0	0.30	0.30 ⎱	*
		9.5	0.20	0.30 ⎰	
		10.0	0.10	0.20	
3. School	5.5	5.7	0.80	0.16	
		5.9	0.40	0.16	
		6.1	0.30	0.18	*
		6.3	0.10	0.08	
4. Shopping	3.0	3.2	0.60	0.12	
mall		3.4	0.40	0.16	*
		3.6	0.10	0.06	

badly do they need the work? How are they likely to estimate and bid the jobs? How do our (Bildenhire's) chances of being the low bidder on each job depend upon our bid? ... and so on.

Table 6.1 summarizes the best collective judgment of Bildenhire's managers. For example, management decided that it had no interest in submitting a bid below $11.0 million for the office building, and that a bid in excess of $12.5 million had virtually no chance of winning. Therefore, they chose to divide this range into four bid levels corresponding to bids of $11.0, $11.5, $12.0, and $12.5 million. (Of course, they could have chosen intervals of one-tenth or one-quarter million dollars, if it seemed useful.) Then they judged that a bid of $11.0 million had a six-tenths (0.6) chance of being the low bid, and so on.

The *chance-of-winning* estimates are subjective. Although the managers would have preferred some objective means of determining these, they recognized that the market place is constantly changing, and data from previous contracts might not reflect current conditions. Their "feel for the market," however, includes up-to-date information and a shrewd assessment of competition.

Since Bildenhire's managers could not work directly with profit, they adopted the idea of *chance-weighted profit* (C-W-P), that is, the estimated profit multiplied by the chance of winning. For example, if the bid of $11.0 million for the office project should be a winner, the estimated profit would be $11.0 − $10.5 million, or $0.5 million. The C-W-P of that bid is

$$0.60 \qquad \times \qquad \$0.5 \text{ million} \quad = .30 \text{ million}$$
$$\text{(chance of winning)} \quad \text{(potential profit)} \quad \text{(C-W-P)}$$

The other C-W-P figures are computed similarly and appear in the last column of Table 6.1.

Having calculated all the C-W-Ps, it appears that the optimal bids are at hand. That is, if a contract is to be bid at all, it should be bid at the level that yields the largest C-W-P (the starred figures in the C-W-P column of Table 6.1). This would be the case if there were no bid bond limitation ($\leq\$18$ million). Because of this restriction, Bildenhire may find it advantageous to bid a contract at a less than optimum, but positive, C-W-P. Bid levels above those yielding the largest C-W-P will have a higher bid bond cost and provide less C-W-P. Therefore, Bildenhire's management decides these need not be considered further. Also, because of bid bond cost, the $9 million bid for the apartment is superior to that of $9.5 million; thus the latter bid is disregarded. The $5.9 million bid for the school is deleted for similar reasons.

Bildenhire's management is now prepared to formulate its decision problem. The program is similar to that used by Stack & Bricks in the previous section, except that it accounts for different bid levels. First, define zero–one variables X_{ij} to represent the jth bid on the ith contract. (In this case, $j = 1, 2$ for each $i = 1, 2, 3, 4$, since each contract has two remaining bids to consider.) Each X_{ij} variable should equal unity if a bid (on project i) is to be made at bid level j and zero otherwise. For example, if X_{11} and X_{12} represent the $11.0 and $11.5 million bids on the office project, and if the solution indicates that $\{X_{11} = 0$ and $X_{12} = 1\}$, then the bid should be $11.5 million. Of course, if both variables equal zero, the project should not be bid.

An equation for the total C-W-P can then be written:

$$\text{C-W-P}_{\text{total}} = 0.30X_{11} + 0.40X_{12} + 0.25X_{21} + 0.30X_{22} + 0.16X_{31}$$
$$+ 0.18X_{32} + 0.12X_{41} + 0.16X_{42}$$

in millions of dollars. Bildenhire's managers could choose an objective that maximizes this quantity. However, they feel it more appropriate to maximize an adjusted C-W-P equation which accounts for bid bond costs, that is:

maximize:

$$Z' = \{\text{C-W-P}_{\text{total}}\} - 0.022X_{11} - 0.023X_{12} - 0.017X_{21} - 0.018X_{22}$$
$$- 0.0114X_{31} - 0.0122X_{32} - 0.0064X_{41} - 0.0068X_{42}$$

where the coefficients of X_{ij} are the products of the bid bond rate ($0.002 million per million dollars) and the corresponding bids (in millions of dollars). This objective equation can be simplified as:

maximize:

$$Z = 278X_{11} + 377X_{12} + 233X_{21} + 282X_{22} + 159X_{31} + 178X_{32}$$
$$+ 114X_{41} + 153X_{42}$$

whose coefficients are rounded to the nearest thousand dollars. Here, of course, the units of Z are thousands of dollars.

Since there is to be, at most, one bid per contract, the following constraints are necessary:

$$X_{11} + X_{12} \leq 1 \qquad \text{office bids}$$

$$X_{21} + X_{22} \leq 1 \qquad \text{apartment bids}$$

$$X_{31} + X_{32} \leq 1 \qquad \text{school bids}$$

$$X_{41} + X_{42} \leq 1 \qquad \text{mall bids}$$

Resource constraints are needed for the limited number of tower cranes, air compressors, and crawler tractors. Since only four tower cranes are available, and two are required for the first two projects and one for the third, write:

$$2X_{11} + 2X_{12} + 2X_{21} + 2X_{22} + 1X_{31} + 1X_{32} \leq 4 \qquad \text{(cranes)}$$

Each project requires one air compressor and three are available. Therefore:

$$X_{11} + X_{12} + X_{21} + X_{22} + X_{31} + X_{32} + X_{41} + X_{42} \leq 3 \qquad \text{(compressors)}$$

Each project also requires a crawler tractor. Only two are available, but one can be shared between the school and mall projects. Two constraints are used to describe this possibility:

$$X_{11} + X_{12} + X_{21} + X_{22} + X_{31} + X_{32} \leq 2$$

and $\qquad\qquad\qquad\qquad\qquad\qquad\qquad\qquad\qquad$ (tractors)

$$X_{11} + X_{12} + X_{21} + X_{22} + X_{41} + X_{42} \leq 2$$

These constraints accomplish their purpose because if both the office and the apartment projects are bid, then the quantity

$$[X_{11} + X_{12} + X_{21} + X_{22}]$$

will equal 2 (indicating that two crawler tractors may be required). Therefore, X_{31}, X_{32}, X_{41}, and X_{42} must be zero, that is, neither the school nor the mall project can be bid. However, if the office and apartment projects are not both bid, the above quantity (in brackets) will equal at most unity, and the constraints allow bidding both the school and the mall projects.

Finally, the bonding restriction requires that the sum total of submitted bids be no greater than $18 million. Therefore,

$$11.0X_{11} + 11.5X_{12} + 8.5X_{21} + 9.0X_{22} + 5.7X_{31} + 6.1X_{32}$$
$$+ 3.2X_{41} + 3.4X_{42} \leq 18$$

Of course, the coefficients equal the corresponding bids of each X_{ij}.

Since the adjusted C-W-P objective equation and the constraints are linear, Bildenhire's problem can be solved as a linear program with integer (zero–one) variables. The solution, in Display 6.4, indicates:

$$X_{21} = 1, \qquad X_{32} = 1, \qquad X_{42} = 1$$

and all other variables equal zero. That is, if the apartment project is bid for $8.5 million, the school for $6.1 million, and the mall for $3.4 million, the maximum adjusted C-W-P, Z^*, equals $564,000.

Bildenhire's management observes that an increase in their exposure limit could have a marked effect on their anticipated profit. Suppose that the bonding company is willing to increase the exposure limit from $18 million to a maximum of $21 million at the increased rate of 1.2% ($12,000 per $1 million) for bid bond amounts over $18 million.

To study the effect of this opportunity, revise the original formulation by first defining a variable B to represent the increase in exposure limit (in millions of dollars). Since the total allowable bid bond is now $(18 + B)$

```
FORMULATION:

MAXIMIZE Z = 278 X11 + 377 X12 + 233 X21 + 282 X22 + 159 X31 +
                178 X32 + 114 X41 + 153 X42

SUBJECT TO:

X11 + X12 <= 1
X21 + X22 <= 1
X31 + X32 <= 1
X41 + X42 <= 1
2X11 + 2X12 + 2X21 + 2X22 + X31 + X32                <= 4 (CRANES)
 X11 +  X12 +  X21 +  X22 + X31 + X32 + X41 + X42 <= 3 (COMPRESSORS)
 X11 +  X12 +  X21 +  X22 + X31 + X32             <= 2 (TRACTORS)
 X11 +  X12 +  X21 +  X22 +             X41 + X42 <= 2 (TRACTORS)
11.0X11 + 11.5X12 + 8.5X21 + 9.0X22 + 5.7X31 +
                    6.1X32 + 3.2X41 + 3.4X42      <=18 ($ BOND)

AND X11, X12, X21, ..., X41 AND X42 NON-NEGATIVE AND INTEGER.


SOLUTION:

            CHANCE-WEIGHTED-PROFIT, Z = 564.0
                   X11 = 0.0        X31 = 0.0
                   X12 = 0.0        X32 = 1.0
                   X21 = 1.0        X41 = 0.0
                   X22 = 0.0        X42 = 1.0
```

Display 6.4. Linear programming formulation and solution for Bildenhire's bid decision.

million, the bid bond constraint becomes:

$$11.0X_{11} + 11.5X_{12} + 8.5X_{21} + \cdots + 3.4X_{42} \leq 18 + B$$

or, equivalently,

$$11.0X_{11} + 11.5X_{12} + 8.5X_{21} + \cdots + 3.4X_{42} - B \leq 18$$

The objective equation must be modified to account for additional bid bond costs, that is:

maximize:

$$Z = 278X_{11} + 377X_{12} + 233X_{21} + \cdots + 153X_{42} - 10B$$

(in thousands of dollars). The coefficient of B is 10 (thousand) because this is the *increase* above the normal bid bond cost. Recall that the normal cost — or 0.2% ($2000 per million) — had already been subtracted for the adjusted C-W-P equation.

Finally, the additional constraint

$$B \leq 3 \text{ (million)}$$

completes the modification to account for the increased exposure limit.

Since the variable B is nonnegative (≥ 0), but not necessarily integer, this revised problem is called a *mixed-integer linear program*. It appears with its solution in Display 6.5. Given an opportunity to increase its allowable bid bond to $21 million, Bildenhire should bid the office, school,

```
FORMULATION:

MAXIMIZE Z = 278 X11 + 377 X12 + 233 X21 + 282 X22 + 159 X31 +
             178 X32 + 114 X41 + 153 X42 - 10 B

SUBJECT TO:

X11 + X12 <= 1
X21 + X22 <= 1
X31 + X32 <= 1
X41 + X42 <= 1
2X11 + 2X12 + 2X21 + 2X22 + X31 + X32                 <= 4 (CRANES)
 X11 +  X12 +  X21 +  X22 + X31 + X32 + X41 + X42 <= 3 (COMPRESSORS)
 X11 +  X12 +  X21 +  X22 + X31 + X32             <= 2 (TRACTORS)
 X11 +  X12 +  X21 +  X22 +             X41 + X42 <= 2 (TRACTORS)
11.0X11 + 11.5X12 + 8.5X21 + 9.0X22 + 5.7X31 +
                    6.1X32 + 3.2X41 + 3.4X42 - B   <=18 ($ BOND)
    B <= 3

AND B NON-NEGATIVE; X11, ..., X42 NON-NEGATIVE AND INTEGER.

SOLUTION:

              CHANCE-WEIGHTED-PROFIT, Z = 678.0

              X11 = 0.0    X22 = 0.0    X41 = 0.0
              X12 = 1.0    X31 = 0.0    X42 = 1.0
              X21 = 0.0    X32 = 1.0    B   = 3.0
```

Display 6.5. Linear programming formulation and solution for Bildenhire's bid decision with an increased exposure limit.

and mall projects, all at their maximum C-W-P values. In this case, the maximum adjusted C-W-P is Z^* which equals \$678,000, confirming management's judgment to seek the increased exposure limit. The computational cost for solving the formulation in Display 6.5 was 44¢ on the Burroughs B7700 computer.

An attractive feature of this formulation for a competitive decision process is that it utilizes a manager's hunches and intuition about the chances of winning. Once again, linear programming is relied upon to keep track of resources and selection alternatives while determining those that are optimum. The linear program can perform this task infallibly. However, other aspects of the formulation still require careful managerial attention.

For example, recall the previous solution which called for bidding on the office, school, and mall projects. The optimal bid for the office project is \$11.5 million, and Bildenhire's management judged that it has a four-tenths chance of winning. The optimal bids for the school and mall projects have three-tenths and four-tenths chances of winning, respectively. Said another way, these respective bids have six-tenths, seven-tenths, and six-tenths chances of losing. Thus there is a very good chance that all three air compressors will not be required for these projects simply because not all three bids will probably be "winners." However, even if the bid bond and supplies of other resources were sufficient, the apartment project could not be chosen because of the compressor constraint. But if at least one of the three compressors is likely to be available, Bildenhire should also consider bidding the apartment project.

The point is that an implicit assumption in the previous analysis is that necessary equipment (cranes, compressors, and tractors) could not be overcommitted. Such an absolute limit is realistic for some high-expense specialized equipment such as heavy-duty cranes, portable batch plants, or crane barges which are not readily available elsewhere. However, when additional equipment or other resources can be obtained elsewhere and at reasonable expense, competitive situations require probabilistic modeling techniques that are beyond the scope here. Interested readers should consult the references in Appendix 5.

Another point is that it is no more likely that the C-W-P will be the actual profit than that every 100 tosses of a coin will yield the average number of 50 heads. Since the actual or "in-pocket" profit cannot be known in advance, a surrogate objective is required, and maximization of C-W-P can be a sensible one.

The solutions obtained to the linear program or any other formulation should be regarded as an aid to, not a replacement for, competent managerial decisions. Assessment of financial capacity, resource availability, and acceptable levels of risk are only a few of the judgments still required of managers.

CHAPTER 7

UNIT PRICE PROPOSALS

I. Bidwell is preparing a bid for excavation work on the *unit price proposal* shown in Table 7.1.

Based upon experience, Bidwell determines *unit costs* and adds a 5% markup to obtain the *unit prices*. These are multiplied by the proposal quantities, and the results are summed to determine the total bid of $262,500 (see Table 7.2).

Bidwell is familiar with unit price proposals since much construction is tendered in that way. If he is awarded the contract, he will be paid

TABLE 7.1.   Unit Price Proposal Format

Item	Description	Quantity	Unit Price	Item Total
1	Clear and grub	20,000 yd^2		
2	Earth excavation	75,000 yd^3		
3	Rock excavation	25,000 yd^3		
4	Cleanup	20,000 yd^2		
			Bid total =	

TABLE 7.2.   Bidwell's Bid Data

Item	Unit Cost	Unit Price	Proposal Quantities	Item Total
1	$2.00/yd^2	$2.10/yd^2	20,000 yd^2	$42,000
2	$1.00/yd^3	$1.05/yd^3	75,000 yd^3	$78,750
3	$3.80/yd^3	$3.99/yd^3	25,000 yd^3	$99,750
4	$2.00/yd^2	$2.10/yd^2	20,000 yd^2	$42,000
			Bid total =	$262,500

periodically (usually monthly) for in-place measured work at the unit price. A percentage of each payment, called *retainage* (usually 10%), will be withheld until the project is completed and accepted. It is Bidwell's responsibility (and expense) to obtain funds which, with the periodic payments, are adequate to set up and execute the job.

Bidwell has a *cash-flow* problem. He senses that if he arranges his unit prices so that items completed early in the project are priced a bit higher and those that occur later are correspondingly lowered, his cash flow would be improved. In short, Bidwell is considering an *unbalancing* of his bid.

To formulate Bidwell's situation more precisely, a means of measuring cash flow is needed. The next section develops a popular method.

7.1. PRESENT WORTH CASH FLOW

Given two sums of money simultaneously, they can be accurately and unambiguously compared. The key word is simultaneously. When the same monies are disbursed at different times, comparisons can be ambiguous. The basic reason is that, quite apart from such distorting factors as inflation and deflation, money has the ability to earn money. Therefore, "early" money has an advantage over money received at a later time. Of the many ways devised to measure money distributed in time (that is, cash flow), the simplest and most popular method is known as *present worth*.

Imagine that an amount P is invested today at a rate of r dollars per dollar (invested) per month. At the end of 1 month, the value of the investment will be:

$$P + rP = (1 + r)P$$

At the end of 2 months, it will have grown to:

$$(1 + r)P + r\{(1 + r)P\} = (1 + r)^2P$$

representing the value at the end of the first month plus the yield on that amount during the second month. Using similar logic, after t months, the original amount P becomes V, where

$$V = (1 + r)^t P$$

In other words, an amount V to be obtained t months hence has a present worth of:

$$P = \frac{V}{(1 + r)^t}$$

Let us apply this to project revenues. Suppose that a T-month project pays C_1 dollars at the end of the first month, C_2 dollars at the end of the second month, and so on. The total dollar payment is, of course:

$$C = C_1 + C_2 + \cdots + C_T$$

Since monies received in the earlier months are valued more on a unit basis than those received later, the total dollar payment C is not the effective amount received. The present worth of this cash flow is:

$$\frac{C_1}{(1 + r)} + \frac{C_2}{(1 + r)^2} + \cdots + \frac{C_T}{(1 + r)^T}$$

which, of course, is less than C.

Example 1. Project Cash Flow

A contractor expects to receive a total of $1 million for a job over the next 10 months. Estimates of monthly payments (receipts) for completed work are:

Month	Receipts	Month	Receipts
1	$ 60,000	6	$120,000
2	90,000	7	140,000
3	110,000	8	90,000
4	80,000	9	65,000
5	100,000	10	145,000

(10% retainage has been reimbursed in the tenth month.)

Assuming a 1% monthly money rate (that is, $r = 0.01$), the present worth of the contractor's receipts is:

$$\frac{60,000}{(1.01)} + \frac{90,000}{(1.01)^2} + \cdots + \frac{65,000}{(1.01)^9} + \frac{145,000}{(1.01)^{10}} = \$943,861$$

That is, receiving $943,861 now is equivalent, in a present worth sense, to obtaining the $1 million of (estimated) contract receipts disbursed throughout the project's duration.

The present worth of a contractor's expenditures would be calculated in the same way. The difference between the present worth of revenues and the present worth of expenditures is the present worth of (the contractor's) profit.

7.2. FORMULATING BIDWELL'S PROBLEM

Bidwell, true to his name, seeks unit prices that maximize his cash flow while retaining the competitiveness of his bid total. Based upon the quantity estimates, Bidwell determines the duration and completion times of each item listed in the proposal. These are shown in Table 7.3.

TABLE 7.3. Bidwell's Project Schedule Data

Item	Description	Estimated Duration	Completion Time (after start)
1	Clear and grub	2 months	2 months
2	Earth excavation	8 months	10 months
3	Rock excavation	8 months	10 months
4	Cleanup	2 months	12 months

Now suppose, for simplicity, that Bidwell uses a 1% monthly rate for money and that he will be paid in full for each item as it is completed, that is, there is no retainage. Then if X_1 represents the (to be determined) unit price for the first item, X_2 that for the second item, and so on, his cash flow value will be:

$$Z = (1.01)^{-2}20,000X_1 + (1.01)^{-10}75,000X_2$$
$$+ (1.01)^{-10}25,000X_3 + (1.01)^{-12}20,000X_4$$
$$\doteq 19,606X_1 + 67,897X_2 + 22,632X_3 + 17,749X_4$$

Of course, Bidwell desires to maximize Z.

To preserve his bid total, Bidwell forms the constraint:

$$20,000X_1 + 75,000X_2 + 25,000X_3 + 20,000X_4 = \$262,500$$

Also, Bidwell notes that both earth and rock are to be excavated and that the unit price of the former should not exceed that of the latter. In symbols,

$$X_2 - X_3 \leq 0$$

Finally, the unit prices cannot be negative, that is:

$$X_1, X_2, X_3, X_4 \geq 0$$

As stated, Bidwell's problem is a linear program whose solution, by inspection, is:

$$X_1 = \$13.12\tfrac{1}{2}, \qquad X_2 = X_3 = X_4 = 0$$

and

$$Z^* = \$257,329$$

While this solution maximizes cash flow, the unit prices at zero could invite unwanted risks. For one, a tender with zero unit prices could be discarded as erroneous. For another, should the actual quantities be significantly greater than the estimated quantities, the contractor could be required to absorb the expense. At the other extreme, unreasonably high unit prices can also be awkward for much the same reasons. Simple constraints can alleviate these situations.

Suppose that Bidwell decides upon these limits:

$$\$1.00 \leq X_1 \leq \$4.00$$

$$0.50 \leq X_2 \leq 3.00$$

$$1.50 \leq X_3 \leq 6.00$$

$$1.00 \leq X_4 \leq 4.00$$

These constraints are included in Bidwell's linear program, shown in Display 7.1.

The maximum present worth $\{Z^* = \$243,283\}$ is, as expected, less than the previous one since the effect of added constraints is to diminish the possible solutions. However, this value is larger than the present worth that would be obtained using the uniform 5% markup in Table 7.2. The

```
#
RUN $DELIBR/LP
#RUNNING 2993
TYPE HELP IF YOU NEED IT
-->   #?
LOAD
ENTER OBJECTIVE FUNCTION:
OBJ*FN: MAX 19606 X1 + 67897 X2 + 22632 X3 + 17749 X4
ENTER CONSTRAINTS:
CON1:       20000 X1 + 75000 X2 + 25000 X3 + 20000 X4 = 262500
CON2:       X2 - X3 <= 0
CON3:       X1 >= 1.00
CON4:       X1 <= 4.00
CON5:       X2 >= 0.50
CON6:       X2 <= 3.00
CON7:       X3 >= 1.50
CON8:       X3 <= 6.00
CON9:       X4 >= 1.00
CON10:      X4 <= 4.00
CON11:
-->   NONE
-->   SOLVE

OBJECTIVE FUNCTION ATTAINS A MAXIMUM VALUE OF 243282.625 AT:
            X3 =          1.62
            X2 =          1.62
            X1 =          4.00
            X4 =          1.00

-->   STOP
```

Display 7.1. Bidwell's linear program and solution.

present worth in that case is obtained by substituting those unit prices into Bidwell's objective equation, giving $Z = \$240,039$.

7.3. WHEN QUANTITIES VARY

Bidwell knows from experience that actual quantities frequently vary from the estimated quantities listed in a proposal. Since receipts are based upon actual quantities (multiplied by unit prices), such variations have an obvious impact on his cash flow. Prudent contractors, therefore, often make a site survey.

In conducting a site survey on this project, Bidwell concludes that the actual quantities of earth and rock excavation are likely to be closer to 60,000 and 40,000 cubic yards, respectively. Altering the objective equation to reflect these estimates, Bidwell obtains:

maximize:

$$Z = (1.01)^{-2}20,000X_1 + (1.01)^{-10}60,000X_2$$
$$+ (1.01)^{-10}40,000X_3 + (1.01)^{-12}20,000X_4$$
$$\doteq 19,606X_1 + 54,317X_2 + 36,211X_3 + 17,749X_4$$

The coefficients of the bid constraint do not change because his bid will still be based upon the proposal quantities. Also, the relationship between the unit prices for earth and rock excavation is still desired. Therefore, using the same constraints as before, Display 7.2 shows the solution to this linear program as:

$$X_1 = 2.75, \quad X_2 = 0.50, \quad X_3 = 6.00, \quad X_4 = 1.00$$

and

$$Z^* = \$316,090$$

If Bidwell's estimates are good ones, the present worth using these unit prices is substantially greater than the present worth with the unit prices in Table 7.2, that is:

$$19,606(2.10) + 54,317(1.05) + 36,211(3.99) + 17,749(2.10)$$
$$= \$279,960$$

7.4. LINEAR PROGRAMMING FORMULATION
FOR UNIT PRICE PROPOSALS

It is useful to formalize Bidwell's situation into a general one. Consider a unit price proposal containing N items with an estimated project duration of T months for which a competitive total bid B has been determined.

```
#
RUN $DELIBR/LP
#RUNNING 2995
TYPE HELP IF YOU NEED IT
-->  #?
LOAD
ENTER OBJECTIVE FUNCTION:
OBJ*FN: MAX 19606 X1 + 54317 X2 + 36211 X3 + 17749 X4
ENTER CONSTRAINTS:
CON1:         20000 X1 + 75000 X2 + 25000 X3 + 20000 X4 = 262500
CON2:         X2 - X3 <= 0
CON3:         X1 >= 1.00
CON4:         X1 <= 4.00
CON5:         X2 >= 0.50
CON6:         X2 <= 3.00
CON7:         X3 >= 1.50
CON8:         X3 <= 6.00
CON9:         X4 >= 1.00
CON10:        X4 <= 4.00
CON11:
-->  NONE
-->  SOLVE


OBJECTIVE FUNCTION ATTAINS A MAXIMUM VALUE OF 316090 AT:
              X3 =         6.00
              X1 =         2.75
              X2 =         0.50
              X4 =         1.00

-->  STOP
```

Display 7.2. Bidwell's linear program and solution with adjusted quantities.

Unit prices are to be determined so that cash flow is maximized while retaining the integrity of the tender.

Forming a project schedule, let $q(n, t)$ be the quantity of the nth item $(n = 1, 2, \ldots, N)$ to be completed in the tth month $(t = 1, 2, \ldots, T)$. Of course, the sum of $q(n, t)$ over t for each item, that is:

$$q(n, 1) + q(n, 2) + \cdots + q(n, T)$$

should equal Q_n, the contractor's quantity estimate for that item. (This total may or may not be equal to the quantity estimate Q_n in the proposal.) Also, define a discount factor v equal to $(1 + r)^{-1}$, where r is the monthly money rate. Then, using X_n as the unit price for the nth item and a retainage rate of $(1 - a) \times 100\%$, the objective equation for maximizing present worth is written:

maximize:

$$
\begin{aligned}
Z = &\{av^1 q(1, 1) + av^2 q(1, 2) + \cdots + av^T q(1, T) + (1 - a)v^T Q_1\}X_1 \\
+ &\{av^1 q(2, 1) + av^2 q(2, 2) + \cdots + av^T q(2, T) + (1 - a)v^T Q_2\}X_2 \\
&+ \cdots \\
+ &\{av^1 q(N, 1) + av^2 q(N, 2) + \cdots + av^T q(N, T) + (1 - a)v^T Q_N\}X_N
\end{aligned}
$$

$$(1)$$

where a is the fractional payment rate. Here retainage is assumed to be paid upon completion of the job (at the end of period T).

One limitation upon the unit prices is that when they are multiplied by the proposed item quantities Q'_n, they sum to the bid total B, that is:

$$Q'_1 X_1 + Q'_2 X_2 + \cdots + Q'_N X_N = B \qquad (2)$$

This is called the *bid constraint*.

Another source of constraints arises in bounding the unit prices to protect against quantity alterations and contract deletions. If L_n and U_n denote respective lower and upper bounds on the unit price for the nth item,

$$X_n \geq L_n$$

$$X_n \leq U_n, \qquad n = 1, 2, \ldots, N \qquad (3)$$

These are called *bound constraints*.

Since a contractor can repudiate bids in case of an obvious mistake, clients routinely screen bids for errors. For example, as noted earlier, a unit price for earth excavation has the appearance of error if it exceeds the unit price for rock excavation since the latter is more costly. In such a situation, a *formality constraint* can be written as:

$$X_e - X_r \leq 0 \qquad (4)$$

where X_e and X_r represent the respective unit prices for earth and rock excavation.

When the timing of revenues is useful, say, for tax advantage or client convenience, a *timing constraint* can be included in the formulation. The constraint

$$a\{q(1,1) + q(1,2) + \cdots + q(1,t)\} X_1$$
$$+ \ a\{q(2,1) + q(2,2) + \cdots + q(2,t)\} X_2 + \cdots$$
$$+ \ a\{q(N,1) + q(N,2) + \cdots + q(N,t)\} X_N \leq R \qquad (5)$$

restricts the total revenue received during the first t months of a project to a sum R, which may equal a limit on taxable income or a percentage of total revenue anticipated (i.e., if $R = \alpha \sum_{i=1}^{N} Q_i X_i$, $0 \leq \alpha \leq 1$).

Finally, the nonnegativity condition for the unit prices is

$$X_n \geq 0, \qquad n = 1, 2, \ldots, N \qquad (6)$$

The solution to the linear program of Eqs. (1)–(6) provides unit prices that maximize cash flow while retaining the integrity of the tender. Of course, there may be alternative optima which can be examined for preferential selections. However, for the given project information, no other solutions can yield a greater present worth for the project revenues since solutions to linear programs are globally optimal.

The next two examples illustrate the use of the above formulation as well as certain characteristics of bidding and estimating for actual unit price proposals.

Example 2. Bid Proposal for Aqueduct Construction

The advertisement in Table 7.4 was solicited some years ago and brought sealed bids from five contractors. They have been named contractors A, B, C, D, and E in Table 7.5, which includes their unit prices and total bids. Contractor A was awarded the contract based upon his low bid of \$54,068.75. However, note the variations in unit prices. Seasoned bidders are not surprised that the unit prices range, say, for item 1 from \$1000 to \$6000, or for item 4 from \$1.75 to \$8.00, and so on. These variations are typical and cannot be explained solely on the basis of direct costs. Apparently Bidwell, in the last example, was not the first to seek advantageous unit prices.

To illustrate the unbalancing method of the last section, a project completion schedule was fabricated. Table 7.6 represents the quantity of each item completed in the indicated time period (month). The proposal quantities were assumed accurate. For example, 80% of item 1 was completed in the first month and 20% in the second. Therefore, $q(1, 1) = 0.80$, $q(1, 2) = 0.20$, and $q(1, 3) = 0$. For item 2, $q(2, 1) = 140$ cubic yards, $q(2, 2) = 140$ cubic yards, and $q(2, 3) = 0$, and so on.

Using an annual money rate of 12%, so that $r = 0.01$ and $v = 0.99$, and assuming a 10% retainage (i.e., $a = 0.9$), the present worth of future revenue is:

$$
\begin{aligned}
Z = \quad &\{(0.9)(0.99)(0.8) + (0.9)(0.99)^2(0.2) &&+ (0.1)(0.99)^3(1)\}X_1 \\
&+ \{(0.9)(0.99)(140) + (0.9)(0.99)^2(140) &&+ (0.1)(0.99)^3(280)\}X_2 \\
&+ \{(0.9)(0.99)(300) + (0.9)(0.99)^2(500) &&+ (0.1)(0.99)^3(800)\}X_3 \\
&+ \{ \qquad\quad + (0.9)(0.99)^2(400) + (0.9)(0.99)^3(200) + (0.1)(0.99)^3(600)\}X_4 \\
&\qquad\qquad\qquad\qquad\qquad \vdots \\
&+ \{ \qquad\quad + (0.9)(0.99)^2(1200) &&+ (0.1)(0.99)^3(1200)\}X_{14} \\
&+ \{(0.9)(0.99)(0.6) + (0.9)(0.99)^2(0.4) &&+ (0.1)(0.99)^3(1)\}X_{15} \\
= \quad &0.99X_1 + 275.38X_2 + 785.90X_3 + 585.60X_4 + 17.55X_5 + 203.70X_6 + 286.15X_7 \\
&+ 305.34X_8 + 504.57X_9 + 1022.10X_{10} + 15.81X_{11} + 0.58X_{12} + 2619.00X_{13} \\
&+ 1174.80X_{14} + 0.98X_{15}
\end{aligned}
$$

Of course the objective is to maximize this value of Z.

Since contractor A chose a bid of \$54,068.75, the bid constraint is:

$$
\begin{aligned}
1.0X_1 &+ 280X_2 + 800X_3 + 600X_4 + 18X_5 + 210X_6 + 295X_7 + 312X_8 \\
&+ 516X_9 + 1050X_{10} + 16X_{11} + 0.6X_{12} + 2700X_{13} + 1200X_{14} \\
&+ 1.0X_{15} = 54{,}068.75
\end{aligned}
$$

TABLE 7.4. Bid Items for Aqueduct Construction
Removal of Existing Timber Bridges and Placement of Reinforced Concrete Pipes
Completion Date: 60 Working Days

Item	Quantity	Item
1	1 lump sum	Clearing and grubbing
2	280 yd^3	Channel excavation
3	800 yd^3	Excavation for pipe trenches
4	600 yd^3	Select borrow
5	18 ton	Coarse aggregate
6	210 gal	Rc-70 asphalt
7	295 gal	Rc-250 asphalt
8	312 lineal ft	60-inch reinforced concrete pipe
9	516 lineal ft	72-inch reinforced concrete pipe
10	1050 lineal ft	Wire rope guard fence
11	16 each	End post attachments
12	0.6 acre	Seeding
13	2700 yd^2	Mulching
14	1200 yd^2	Riprap (grouted)
15	1 lump sum	Removal of existing structures

TABLE 7.5. Public Record of Bids

	Bidder				
Item	A*	B	C	D	E
1	$1,000.00	$1,000.00	$1,500.00	$5,000.00	$6,000.00
2	1.40	2.00	3.00	1.00	3.00
3	1.40	4.00	6.00	1.50	3.50
4	1.75	3.00	3.50	3.50	8.00
5	50.00	15.00	10.00	80.00	25.00
6	0.75	0.25	0.20	0.80	1.00
7	0.75	0.25	0.20	0.80	1.00
8	26.50	30.00	33.00	38.00	38.00
9	44.00	45.00	55.00	53.00	50.00
10	2.20	2.50	2.60	2.50	2.10
11	86.00	100.00	100.00	100.00	82.00
12	500.00	1,000.00	600.00	1,000.00	2,000.00
13	0.10	0.10	0.15	0.25	0.20
14	10.00	12.00	11.00	12.00	11.00
15	2,000.00	2,500.00	4,000.00	5,000.00	5,000.00
Total bids	$54,068.75	$61,531.25	$70,492.00	$74,528.00	$76,508.00

*Winner.

TABLE 7.6. Project Completion Schedule

Item	Proposal Quantity	Time Period (Month) 1	2	3
1	1	0.8	0.2	
2	280	140	140	
3	800	300	500	
4	600		400	200
5	18		10	8
6	210			210
7	295			295
8	312	100	100	112
9	516	150	150	216
10	1050	200		850
11	16	16		
12	0.6			0.6
13	2700			2700
14	1200		1200	
15	1	0.6	0.4	

To bound the unit prices, imagine that contractor A writes:

$$\$1000.00 \le X_1 \le \$5000.00$$

$$1.00 \le X_2 \le 3.00$$

$$1.40 \le X_3 \le 4.00$$

$$1.75 \le X_4 \le 4.00$$

$$20.00 \le X_5 \le 60.00$$

$$0.25 \le X_6 \le 1.00$$

$$0.25 \le X_7 \le 1.00$$

$$25.00 \le X_8 \le 35.00$$

$$40.00 \le X_9 \le 55.00$$

$$2.00 \le X_{10} \le 2.75$$

$$80.00 \le X_{11} \le 100.00$$

$$500.00 \le X_{12} \le 1500.00$$

$$0.10 \le X_{13} \le 0.25$$

$$10.00 \le X_{14} \le 12.00$$

$$2000.00 \le X_{15} \le 5000.00$$

Of course, the nonnegativity condition is already satisfied since each unit price has a positive lower bound.

The solution to this linear program appears in Display 7.3. If the

```
#
RUN $DELIBR/LP
#RUNNING 3483
TYPE HELP IF YOU NEED IT
-->  #?
LOAD
ENTER OBJECTIVE FUNCTION:
OBJ*FN: MAX 0.99 X1  + 275.38 X2  + 785.90 X3  + 585.60 X4  +  17.55 X5 +,
           203.70 X6  + 286.15 X7  + 305.34 X8  + 504.57 X9  +1022.10 X10 +,
            15.81 X11 +   0.58 X12 +2619.00 X13 +1174.80 X14 +   0.98 X15
ENTER CONSTRAINTS:
           1 X1 + 280 X2 + 800 X3 + 600 X4 + 18 X5 + 210 X6 + 295 X7 + ,
              312 X8 + 516 X9 + 1050 X10 + 16 X11 + 0.6 X12 +,
                 2700 X13 + 1200 X14 + 1 X15 = 54068.75
CON1:        X1 >= 1000.00
CON2:        X1 <= 5000.00
CON3:        X2 >= 1.00
CON4:        X2 <= 3.00
CON5:        X3 >= 1.40
CON6:        X3 <= 4.00
CON7:        X4 >= 1.75
CON8:        X4 <= 4.00
CON9:        X5 >= 20.00
CON10:       X5 <= 60.00
CON11:       X6 >= 0.25
CON12:       X6 <= 1.00
CON13:       X7 >= 0.25
CON14:       X7 <= 1.00
CON15:       X8 >= 25.00
CON16:       X8 <= 35.00
CON17:       X9 >= 40.00
CON18:       X9 <= 55.00
CON19:       X10 >= 2.00
CON20:       X10 <= 2.75
CON21:       X11 >= 80.00
CON22:       X11 <= 100.00
CON23:       X12 >= 500.00
CON24:       X12 <= 1500.00
CON25:       X13 >= 0.10
CON26:       X13 <= 0.25
CON27:       X14 >= 10.00
CON28:       X14 <= 12.00
CON29:       X15 >= 2000.00
CON30:       X15 <= 5000.00
CON31:
-->  NONE
-->  SOLVE


OBJECTIVE FUNCTION ATTAINS A MAXIMUM VALUE OF 52954.177 AT:
     X8 =       25.00          X11 =       80.00
     X2 =        1.00          X9  =       40.00
     X3 =        1.40          X10 =        2.00
     X4 =        1.75          X12 =      500.00
     X5 =       20.00          X13 =        0.10
     X6 =        0.25          X14 =       10.00
     X7 =        0.25          X15 =     2000.00
     X1 =     4742.50
```

Display 7.3. Linear program and solution for the bid proposal of example 2.

actual job progress was similar to the project schedule in Table 7.6, contractor A received payments with a present worth (using his unit prices in Table 7.5) equal to \$52,906.25, about \$48 less than he could have received with the optimal unit prices of Display 7.3. While this is a small gain, the savings could be made more or less significant simply by altering the limits of the bound constraints. Of course, larger savings will arise from contracts of long duration where the effect of discounting is pronounced.

Example 3. Bid Proposal for Highway Construction

Table 7.7 shows another advertisement for the construction of a state highway. The sealed bids of three contractors, named F, G, and H, appear in Table 7.8.

TABLE 7.7.   Bid Items for Highway Construction
23.06 Miles
18-feet Surface Treated Roadway on 6-inch Soil Cement Base

Item	Proposed Quantity	Item Description
1	1 lump sum	Clearing and grubbing (23.06 miles)
2	1,000 yd^3	Excavation
3	168,400 yd^3	Borrow
4	1,000 yd^3	Select borrow
5	264,500 yd^3	Soil cement base course
6	26,450 barrels	Portland cement
7	178,500 gal	RC-250 asphalt
8	5,100 ton	Coarse aggregate
9	4,800 lineal ft	12-inch reinforced concrete pipe
10	3,800 lineal ft	15-inch reinforced concrete pipe
11	900 lineal ft	18-inch reinforced concrete pipe
12	300 lineal ft	24-inch reinforced concrete pipe
13	350 lineal ft	36-inch reinforced concrete pipe
14	160 lineal ft	42-inch reinforced concrete pipe
15	160 lineal ft	48-inch reinforced concrete pipe
16	60 lineal ft	54-inch reinforced concrete pipe
17	210 lineal ft	60-inch reinforced concrete pipe
18	70 lineal ft	58-inch × 36-inch corrugated metal pipe bituminous coated
19	1 each	Type PW catch basin
20	100 lineal ft	Wire rope guard fence (wood post)
21	4 each	End post attachments
22	20,000 lineal ft	Lateral ditching
23	30 ton	Calcium chloride for dust control
24	220 yd^2	Grouted riprap
25	1 each	Standard junction box
26	1 lump sum	Removal of existing structures
27	121,756 lineal ft	Seeding and mulching
28	23.06 miles	Grading and reshaping roadway

TABLE 7.8.   Public Record of Bids

Item	Contractor		
	F^*	G	H
1	$24,000.00	$26,100.00	$25,600.00
2	.96	1.00	1.00
3	1.02	1.10	1.18
4	2.00	1.50	1.50
5	0.24	0.25	0.26
6	4.85	4.60	4.15
7	0.125	0.14	0.14
8	6.00	6.50	6.00
9	3.00	3.00	3.00
10	5.00	4.00	5.00
11	6.00	5.00	5.50
12	9.00	8.00	7.00
13	14.00	17.00	12.50
14	18.00	20.00	15.00
15	22.00	26.00	18.00
16	28.00	33.00	24.00
17	35.00	37.00	28.00
18	25.00	32.00	24.00
19	300.00	500.00	250.00
20	2.70	3.00	2.65
21	50.00	50.00	45.00
22	0.70	0.90	0.75
23	70.00	50.00	80.00
24	12.00	10.00	10.00
25	300.00	400.00	200.00
26	600.00	1,000.00	1,000.00
27	0.14	0.15	0.14
28	1,800.00	1,500.00	1,800.00
Total bids	$585,946.84	$598,528.40	$600,993.34

*Winner.

Contractor F was awarded the contract based upon his bid of
$585,946.84. His actual project completion schedule, compiled from the
record of payments he received, is shown in Table 7.9. Note that the item
quantities required to complete the project differ from the quantities
listed in the proposal (as they often do). Because of underruns, contractor
F was paid only $553,963.75. Based on a 12% annual money rate and a
10% retainage, the present worth of this sum was $535,896.13.

Suppose that contractor F had conducted his own site survey and
anticipated the variation between proposed and actual quantities.
Expressing this situation as a linear program, the formulation and solution appear in Display 7.4. Here the coefficients in the objective equation
were determined using Eq. (1) with $v = 0.99$ and $a = 0.9$. The bound

TABLE 7.9. Project Completion Schedule

Item	Actual Quantity		Time Period (Months)				
		1	2	3	4	5
1	1.0 lump sum	1.0				
2	2,479 yd^3	273		731		1,475
3	165,266 yd^3	21,484	6,611	75,196	61,975	
4	0 yd^3					
5	257,230 yd^3			106,750	127,329	23,151
6	23,178 barrels			9,735	13,095	348
7	136,437 gal			30,698	105,739	
8	5,168 ton			1,395	3,695	78
9	5,563 lineal ft	334		1,641	2,837	751
10	2,871 lineal ft	459	603	1,464	345	
11	794 lineal ft	246	198	322		28
12	319 lineal ft	42		242	16	19
13	283 lineal ft	139	82	28	27	7
14	177 lineal ft	161				16
15	169 lineal ft	161				8
16	56 lineal ft	56				
17	208 lineal ft	208				
18	61 lineal ft	60				1
19	1 each				1	
20	0 lineal ft					
21	0 each					
22	21,612 lineal ft	12,103	4,754	3,026	216	1,513
23	0.5 ton	0.25		0.25		
24	264 yd^2	119				145
25	1 each				1.0	
26	1 lump sum	1.0				
27	117,629 lineal ft			27,055	90,574	
28	22.7 miles	5	6	9	2.7	

constraints were arbitrarily chosen by using the lowest and highest unit prices for each item among the submitted bids in Table 7.8. Formality constraints were also included to reflect the increase in price with increasing size of reinforced concrete pipe. If contractor F had used the optimal unit prices (summarized in Table 7.10), the present worth of his receipts would have been $540,669.10, almost 1% more than he received.

7.5. SOME FINAL COMMENTS

Most contractors and clients realize the cash flow advantages of unbalancing unit prices. Indeed, clients make project payments only after work is completed. Therefore, the contractor must frequently seek credit

MAXIMIZE PROFIT = .99X1 + 2378.04X2 + 159865.92X3 + 0X4 + 247435.96X5 +
              22312.19X6 + 131119.37X7 + 4967.97X8 + 5351.95X9 + 2789.71X10 +
              774.30X11 + 309.06X12 + 276.82X13 + 173.95X14 + 166.35X15 +
              55.22X16 + 205.09X17 + 60.11X18 + .96X19 + 0X20 + 0X21 +
              21151.88X22 + .49X23 + 255.24X24 + .96X25 + .99X26 +
              113049.71X27 + 22.09X28

SUBJECT TO:

CON1:   1X1 + 1000X2 + 168400X3 + 1000X4 + 264500X5 + 26450X6 +
        178500X7 + 5100X8 + 4800X9 + 3800X10 + 900X11 + 300X12 +
        350X13 + 160X14 + 160X15 + 60X16 + 210X17 + 70X18 + 1X19 +
        100X20 + 4X21 + 20000X22 + 30X23 + 220X24 + 1X25 + 1X26 +
        121756X27 + 23.06X28 = 585946.84

CON2:	X1 >= 24000.00				
CON3:	X1 <= 26100.00				
CON4:	X2 >= 0.96				
CON5:	X2 <= 1.00				
CON6:	X3 >= 1.02	CON26:	X13 >= 12.50	CON46:	X23 >= 50.00
CON7:	X3 <= 1.18	CON27:	X13 <= 17.00	CON47:	X23 <= 80.00
CON8:	X4 >= 1.50	CON28:	X14 >= 15.00	CON48:	X24 >= 10.00
CON9:	X4 <= 2.00	CON29:	X14 <= 20.00	CON49:	X24 <= 12.00
CON10:	X5 >= 0.24	CON30:	X15 >= 18.00	CON50:	X25 >= 200.00
CON11:	X5 <= 0.26	CON31:	X15 <= 26.00	CON51:	X25 <= 400.00
CON12:	X6 >= 4.15	CON32:	X16 >= 24.00	CON52:	X26 >= 600.00
CON13:	X6 <= 4.85	CON33:	X16 <= 33.00	CON53:	X26 <= 1000.00
CON14:	X7 >= 0.125	CON34:	X17 >= 28.00	CON54:	X27 >= 0.14
CON15:	X7 <= 0.14	CON35:	X17 <= 37.00	CON55:	X27 <= 0.15
CON16:	X8 >= 6.00	CON36:	X18 >= 24.00	CON56:	X28 >= 1500.00
CON17:	X8 <= 6.50	CON37:	X18 <= 32.00	CON57:	X28 <= 1800.00
CON18:	X9 >= 3.00	CON38:	X19 >= 250.00	CON58:	X9 - X10 <= 0
CON19:	X9 <= 3.00	CON39:	X19 <= 500.00	CON59:	X10 - X11 <= 0
CON20:	X10 >= 4.00	CON40:	X20 >= 2.65	CON60:	X11 - X12 <= 0
CON21:	X10 <= 5.00	CON41:	X20 <= 3.00	CON61:	X12 - X13 <= 0
CON22:	X11 >= 5.00	CON42:	X21 >= 45.00	CON62:	X13 - X14 <= 0
CON23:	X11 <= 6.00	CON43:	X21 <= 50.00	CON63:	X14 - X15 <= 0
CON24:	X12 >= 7.00	CON44:	X22 >= 0.70	CON64:	X15 - X16 <= 0
CON25:	X12 <= 9.00	CON45:	X22 <= 0.90	CON65:	X16 - X17 <= 0

SOLUTION: PROFIT ATTAINS A MAXIMUM VALUE OF 540669.10 AT:

X1 = 26100.000		X11 = 5.0000		X22 = 0.900	
X2 = 1.000		X12 = 9.0000		X23 = 50.000	
X3 = 1.105		X13 = 12.500		X24 = 12.000	
X5 = 0.240		X14 = 20.000		X25 = 400.000	
X6 = 4.150		X15 = 26.000		X26 = 1000.000	
X7 = 0.125		X16 = 26.000		X27 = 0.140	
X8 = 6.500		X17 = 37.000		X28 = 1800.000	
X9 = 3.000		X18 = 24.000		X4 = 1.500	
X10 = 4.000		X19 = 500.000		X20 = 2.650	
		X21 = 45.000			

Display 7.4. Linear programming formulation and solution for the bid proposal of example 3.

TABLE 7.10. Optimal Unit Prices for
Highway Construction

Item		Item	
1	$26,100.00	15	$ 26.00
2	1.00	16	26.00
3	1.105	17	37.00
4	1.50	18	24.00
5	0.24	19	500.00
6	4.15	20	2.65
7	0.125	21	45.00
8	6.50	22	0.90
9	3.00	23	50.00
10	4.00	24	12.00
11	5.00	25	400.00
12	9.00	26	1,000.00
13	12.50	27	0.14
14	20.00	28	1,800.00

or borrow money to finance the project. Contractors find it advantageous to increase their unit prices on work items scheduled for early completion, while correspondingly decreasing those on items scheduled later in the job. This procedure provides additional early revenues to help the contractor finance later portions of the job without affecting the competitiveness of the overall bid.

Even greater advantages can accrue to contractors who understand the job well. There is the case of one contractor whose knowledge of site conditions enabled him to forecast correctly that trench sheeting, an item in the advertised proposal, would not be needed in the dense soil. He set a 1¢ price on that item, reduced his total bid proportionally, and was the low bidder by an amount comparable to the cost of the trench sheeting.

The unbalancing of unit prices is a common and perhaps necessary practice in the construction industry. The formulation of a linear program for determining the optimal unit prices has the property that for the same project information, no other means of unbalancing can yield a greater present worth of future revenue.

If the objective had been to maximize the present worth of future profit, the objective equation might be written:

maximize:

$$Z_p = Z - \sum_{t=1}^{T'} v^t C_t$$

where Z is the present worth of revenues as defined in Eq. (1). The second term in the above expression represents the present worth of project costs, that is, C_t is the total contract expenditure in period t ($t = 1, 2, \ldots, T'$).

(Note that T' may not equal T since contractor debts may be settled before, or extended beyond, contract payments.) Since this additional cost term does not involve the unit price variables, the optimal values are the same, whether the objective is the present worth of revenue or of profit, as long as the project schedule is the same. However, jobs can be scheduled in several ways, and the cash flows will likely vary among them. When alternative schedules are being compared, the greatest present worth of profits can be determined by comparing the linear programming solutions of all schedules.

Finally, recall that answers to such "what happens if?" questions as "the bid B is increased (or decreased) by $1000," or "the bound constraints on unit prices are altered," or "a timing constraint is included (or excluded, or altered)," and so on, are often available from a sensitivity analysis.

CHAPTER 8

CRITICAL PATH METHOD

Jack M. Up Construction has contracted to complete a one-story building. The job is broken into a dozen simplified tasks in Table 8.1. Normal costs and completion times have been estimated for each task, and precedence relationships among tasks have been noted.

For example, roofing (task *H*) is estimated to cost $10,000 and requires about 2 weeks for completion under normal conditions. Also, roofing cannot begin until the framing, task *F,* is completed.

How should Jack M. Up schedule the tasks to minimize the total job duration?

TABLE 8.1. Jack M. Up's Construction Planning Data

Task	Description	Estimates of		Immediately Preceding Tasks
		Cost ($000)	Completion Time (weeks)	
A	Site preparation	5	2	(Start)
B	Foundation	12	4	*A*
C	Basement utilities	8	2	*B*
D	Decking	8	2	*C*
E	Floor slab	4	3	*D*
F	Framing	8	2	*B*
G	Exterior walls	8	2	*F*
H	Roofing	10	2	*F*
I	Mechanical/electrical	2	1	*H*
J	Ceilings	2	1	*E, G, I*
K	Interior finishing	4	3	*J*
L	Exterior finishing	4	3	*G*

8.1. CRITICAL PATH METHOD (CPM)

Jack M. Up's situation is typical of project scheduling type problems. While there are several possible methodologies for their solution, perhaps the best known is the *critical path method* (CPM). The main ideas are outlined below.

Figure 8.1 translates the project information into a *network* or *flow diagram*. Assume that site preparation begins at time zero, so its *earliest starting time* (EST) equals zero. Site preparation requires 2 weeks and, therefore, could be completed by the end of the second week; therefore, its *earliest finishing time* (EFT) is 2 weeks. The foundation task can begin at completion of site preparation. Therefore, its EST equals 2, and since its completion is estimated to take 4 weeks, its EFT equals 2 + 4 = 6, that is, at the end of the sixth week. Continuing in this manner, the EFTs for the floor slab, mechanical/electrical, and exterior walls are 13, 11, and 10 weeks, respectively. Since work on the ceiling cannot begin until all three of these tasks are completed, the EST of the ceiling task is 13, corresponding to the EFT of the floor slab. Finally, since the EFTs of interior and exterior finishing are 17 and 13, respectively, the earliest the project can be completed is 17 weeks (under normal conditions). These results are tabulated in columns (5) and (6) of Table 8.2.

In a similar way, but tabulating in reverse, one can determine the *latest starting time* (LST) and *latest finishing time* (LFT) for each task if the project is to be completed in 17 weeks. The LSTs and LFTs are listed in columns (7) and (8) of Table 8.2 without further discussion.

The difference between LST and EST (or LFT and EFT) is called the *slack time* for that task. Tasks with zero slack time are said to be on the *critical path*. The reason is that any delay in their completion times causes a corresponding delay in the completion of the entire project. Such tasks form continuous path or paths through the project network (such as the heavier arrows in Figure 8.1). Naturally, a manager is especially alert to circumstances that might affect the completion of tasks on the critical path.

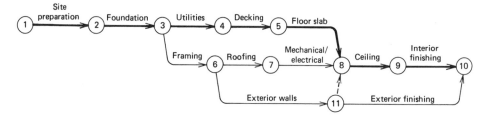

Figure 8.1. Network diagram for Jack M. Up's job.

TABLE 8.2.   CPM Network Analysis for Jack M. Up's Job

Nodes (1)	Task (2)	Description (3)	Duration (4)	EST (5)	EFT (6)	LST (7)	LFT (8)	Slack (9)
1-2	A	Site preparation	2	0	2	0	2	0
2-3	B	Foundation	4	2	6	2	6	0
3-4	C	Basement utilities	2	6	8	6	8	0
4-5	D	Decking	2	8	10	8	10	0
5-9	E	Floor slab	3	10	13	10	13	0
3-6	F	Framing	2	6	8	8	10	2
6-8	G	Exterior walls	2	8	10	11	13	3
6-7	H	Roofing	2	8	10	10	12	2
7-9	I	Mechanical/electrical	1	10	11	12	13	2
9-10	J	Ceiling	1	13	14	13	14	0
10-11	K	Interior finishing	3	14	17	14	17	0
8-11	L	Exterior finishing	3	10	13	14	17	4

EST—earliest starting time; EFT—earliest finishing time; LST—latest starting time; LFT—latest finishing time.

8.2.   LINEAR PROGRAMMING FORMULATION

Recall that Jack M. Up sought to schedule a dozen construction tasks so that the total job duration was a minimum. Let X_A denote the starting time for task A (site preparation), X_B the starting time for task B (foundation), and so on. For convenience, let X_P denote the time to complete the entire project. Then, if Jack M. Up desires to minimize the total job duration, his objective equation is simply:

minimize: $$Z = X_P \qquad (1)$$

The precedence relations among tasks form the constraint equations. For example, work on task B can begin anytime after completion of task A or, equivalently, 2 weeks after the start of task A, that is:

$$X_B \geq X_A + 2$$

or, equivalently,

$$X_B - X_A \geq 2 \qquad (2)$$

Similarly, task C can begin anytime after 4 weeks from the start of task B. Therefore:

$$X_C - X_B \geq 4 \qquad (3)$$

Similarly:

$$X_D - X_C \geq 2 \qquad (4)$$

$$X_E - X_D \geq 2 \qquad (5)$$

$$X_F - X_B \geq 4 \qquad (6)$$

$$X_G - X_F \geq 2 \qquad (7)$$

$$X_H - X_F \geq 2 \qquad (8)$$

$$X_I - X_H \geq 2 \qquad (9)$$

$$X_J - X_E \geq 3 \qquad (10)$$

$$X_J - X_G \geq 2 \qquad (11)$$

$$X_J - X_I \geq 1 \qquad (12)$$

$$X_K - X_J \geq 1 \qquad (13)$$

$$X_L - X_G \geq 2 \qquad (14)$$

$$X_P - X_K \geq 3 \qquad (15)$$

$$X_P - X_L \geq 3 \qquad (16)$$

and, of course,

$$X_A, X_B, \ldots, X_L, X_P \geq 0 \qquad (17)$$

Note that three constraints, Eqs. (10)–(12), each begin with starting time X_J since work on the ceiling (J) cannot begin until the floor slab (E), exterior walls (G), and mechanical/electrical (I) are completed. Similarly, constraint equations (15) and (16) involve X_P because the job is not complete until both exterior and interior finishings, tasks K and L, are accomplished.

The objective equation [Eq. (1)] and the 15 constraint equations [Eqs. (2)–(16)], together with the nonnegativity condition [Eq. (17)], represent a linear optimization problem. The complete formulation and the computer-aided solution appear in Display 8.1. The solution, $X_P = 17$ (weeks), agrees with the CPM analysis. Similarly, the optimal values of $X_A, X_B, \ldots, X_L$ correspond to the earliest start times in Table 8.2. Also, a portion of the sensitivity analysis, Display 8.2, indicates which tasks are not on the critical path [tasks listed in column (1) with a corresponding zero unit cost in column (2)] and contains enough information to determine their respective slack times [equal to the difference between the corresponding finite quantities in columns (3) and (4)].

8.3. SCHEDULING FOR MINIMUM COST

Jack M. Up's management did not anticipate that the job would require 17 weeks under normal conditions. They had contracted to complete the job in 14 weeks. Since this is not possible under normal conditions, they must consider ways to reduce project duration. One possibility is to

```
#
RUN $DELIBR/LP
#RUNNING 0906
TYPE HELP IF YOU NEED IT
-->  #?
LOAD
ENTER OBJECTIVE FUNCTION:
OBJ*FN: MIN   XP
ENTER CONSTRAINTS:
CON1:    XB - XA >= 2
CON2:    XC - XB >= 4
CON3:    XD - XC >= 2
CON4:    XE - XD >= 2
CON5:    XF - XB >= 4
CON6:    XG - XF >= 2
CON7:    XH - XF >= 2
CON8:    XI - XH >= 2
CON9:    XJ - XE >= 3
CON10:   XJ - XG >= 2
CON11:   XJ - XI >= 1
CON12:   XK - XJ >= 1
CON13:   XL - XG >= 2
CON14:   XP - XK >= 3
CON15:   XP - XL >= 3
CON16:
-->  NONE
-->  SOLVE


OBJECTIVE FUNCTION ATTAINS A MINIMUM VALUE OF 17 AT:
                      XB =        2.00
                      XC =        6.00
                      XD =        8.00
                      XE =       10.00
                      XF =        6.00
                      XG =        8.00
                      XH =        8.00
                      XI =       10.00
                      XJ =       13.00
                      XK =       14.00
                      XL =       10.00
                      XP =       17.00

        THE OTHER VARIABLE HAS A VALUE OF ZERO.

-->  STOP
```

Display 8.1. Jack M. Up's formulation and solution to minimize job duration.

employ additional or more efficient resources (say, labor and/or machines) at an increased cost, of course. In this case, management must decide which tasks should be allocated additional resources.

Suppose that management examined each of the 12 construction tasks and found that many could be completed earlier by a *crash* effort at reasonable added expense. Table 8.3 summarizes the results of their analysis. For example, task *A* takes 2 weeks to accomplish under normal conditions and costs $5000. However, with an additional allocation of $3000 ($8000 total) the same task can be completed in 1 week.

(0) CONSTRAINT ROW	(1) LIMITING PROCESS	(2) UNIT COST	(3) LOWER LIMIT	(4) UPPER ACTIVITY
CON1	XB	− 1.000	2.000	INFINITY
CON2	CON11	− 1.000	4.000	INFINITY
CON3	CON11	− 1.000	2.000	INFINITY
CON4	CON11	− 1.000	2.000	INFINITY
CON5	XF	0.000	4.000	6.000
CON6	XG	0.000	2.000	5.000
CON7	XH	0.000	2.000	4.000
CON8	XI	0.000	2.000	4.000
CON9	CON11	− 1.000	3.000	INFINITY
CON12	CON15	− 1.000	1.000	INFINITY
CON13	XL	0.000	2.000	6.000
CON14	CON15	− 1.000	3.000	INFINITY

Display 8.2.   Sensitivity analysis for Jack M. Up's formulation.

Jack M. Up's management did not feel that tasks C, E, I, or J could be shortened at reasonable expense; therefore, crash times and costs are not listed.

Column (8) of Table 8.3 reflects the (average) increase in cost per unit time saved. Simply, it is equal to the additional cost [column (6)] divided by the possible time savings [column (7)].

Instead of minimizing the (normal) project duration X_P, Jack M. Up's objective is now to minimize the cost of completing the project within 14 weeks. Considering the possibility of a crash effort, the cost of task A can be estimated as:

$$C_A \doteq N_A + U_A T_A = \$5000 + \$3000 T_A$$

where N_A is its cost under normal conditions, U_A the increase in cost per week saved under crash conditions [column (8) of Table 8.3], T_A the number of weeks that task A should be compressed, and $\doteq$ means approximately equal. Of course, the new decision variable T_A must be assigned a value between zero and one (the maximum number of weeks that task A can be shortened). Similarly, for task B:

$$C_B \doteq N_B + U_B T_B = \$12,000 + \$2500 T_B$$

where $0 \le T_B \le 2$; and so on for the remaining tasks that can be shortened. Since the total cost is simply the sum of the 12 task costs, the objective equation is written:

minimize:

$$Z' = C_A + C_B + C_C + \cdots + C_l$$
$$= N_A + N_B + N_C + \cdots + N_L + U_A T_A + U_B T_B + \cdots + U_L T_L$$
$$= 75 + 3T_A + 2.5T_B + 3T_D + 2T_F + 1T_G + 2T_H + 2T_K + 1.5T_L$$

or, equivalently, minimize:

$$Z = Z' - 75 = 3T_A + 2.5T_B + \cdots + 2T_K + 1.5T_L. \quad (5)$$

Here, Z' represents the total cost and Z is that portion attributed to the crash effort (in thousands of dollars). There are no T variables corresponding to tasks $C, E, I,$ or J, since management determined that those tasks could not reasonably be shortened.

An obvious constraint for this formulation is:

$$X_P \leq 14$$

since a 14-week schedule is desired. In addition, some of the precedence constraints of the earlier formulation need revision. If additional re-

TABLE 8.3. Comparison of Time and Cost for Normal and Crash Conditions

Task	Description (1)	Normal Conditions		Crash Conditions		Additional Cost ($000) (6)	Time Saved (weeks) (7)	Additional Cost/Time ($000/wk) (8)
		Cost ($000) (2)	Time (weeks) (3)	Cost ($000) (4)	Time (weeks) (5)			
A	Site preparation	5	2	8	1	3	1	3
B	Foundation	12	4	17	2	5	2	2.5
C	Basement utilities	8	2	—	—	—	—	—
D	Decking	8	2	11	1	3	1	3
E	Floor slabs	4	3	—	—	—	—	—
F	Framing	8	2	10	1	2	1	2
G	Exterior walls	8	2	9	1	1	1	1
H	Roofing	10	2	12	1	2	1	2
I	Mechanical/ electrical	2	1	—	—	—	—	—
J	Ceilings	2	1	—	—	—	—	—
K	Interior finishing	4	3	6	2	2	1	2
L	Exterior finishing	4	3	7	1	3	2	1.5

```
#
RUN $DELIBR/LP
#RUNNING 6746
-->   #?
LOAD
ENTER OBJECTIVE FUNCTION:
OBJ*FN:   MIN  3TA + 2.5TB + 3TD + 2TF + 1TG + 2TH + 2TK + 1.5TL
ENTER CONSTRAINTS:
CON1:     XB - XA + TA >= 2
CON2:     XC - XB + TB >= 4
CON3:     XD - XC >= 2
CON4:     XE - XD + TD >= 2
CON5:     XF - XB + TB >= 4
CON6:     XG - XF + TF >= 2
CON7:     XH - XF + TF >= 2
CON8:     XI - XH + TH >= 2
CON9:     XJ - XE >= 3
CON10:    XJ - XG + TG >= 2
CON11:    XJ - XI >= 1
CON12:    XK - XJ >= 1
CON13:    XL - XG + TG >= 2
CON14:    XP - XK + TK >= 3
CON15:    XP - XL + TL >= 3
CON16:    TA <= 1
CON17:    TB <= 2
CON18:    TD <= 1
CON19:    TF <= 1
CON20:    TG <= 1
CON21:    TH <= 1
CON22:    TK <= 1
CON23:    TL <= 2
CON24:    XP <=14
CON25:
-->   NONE
-->   SOLVE

OBJECTIVE FUNCTION ATTAINS A MINIMUM VALUE OF 7 AT:
                   XB =        2.00
                   XC =        4.00
                   XD =        6.00
                   XE =        8.00
                   XF =        4.00
                   XG =        6.00
                   XH =        6.00
                   XI =        8.00
                   XJ =       11.00
                   XK =       12.00
                   XL =        8.00
                   XP =       14.00
                   TB =        2.00
                   TK =        1.00

      ALL OTHER VARIABLES HAVE A VALUE OF ZERO.

-->   STOP
```

Display 8.3.   Jack M. Up's problem to minimize job costs.

sources are allocated to task A, it will take only $(2 - T_A)$ weeks to complete. Therefore, constraint equation (2) is replaced by

$$X_B - X_A \geq 2 - T_A$$

or equivalently,

$$X_B - X_A + T_A \geq 2$$

Also, since the maximum time task A can be shortened is 1 week, an additional constraint:

$$T_A \leq 1$$

is included. Continuing in this manner, the revised linear optimization problem is shown in Display 8.3. Here the values of the new decision variables $T_A, T_B, T_D, \ldots, T_L$ are to be determined in addition to the early start times $X_A, X_B, \ldots, X_L$. The optimal values of the T variables will indicate which tasks should be shortened and by how many weeks.

The revised 14-week schedule is indicated by the computer-aided solution in Display 8.3. The minimum total cost is \$82,000 ($=Z + \$75,000$) when task B is shortened 2 weeks ($T_B = 2$) and task K by 1 week ($T_K = 1$) from their normal durations.

An implicit assumption in the above minimum cost project schedule is that the increase in cost of the crash effort is directly proportional to the time saved from normal conditions. The cost of task B, for example, was $C_B = N_B + U_B T_B$, as shown in Figure 8.2a. In practice, costs typically increase slowly at first, and then more rapidly with successive increments of time saved (see Figure 8.2b). A more accurate representation of the increase in cost is given by, say, the square of the time saved, that is, $C_B = N_B + U_B T_B^2$. Of course, such cost representations are not linear.

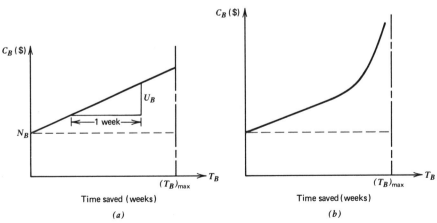

Figure 8.2. Linear and nonlinear time–cost relationships.

Therefore, linear optimization techniques do not apply directly. Approximations can be made to include nonlinear costs in a linear programming formulation. However, the methods are beyond the scope here. Interested readers can consult the references in Appendix 5.

8.4. EXTENSIONS

Jack M. Up's situation is an oversimplified example of project scheduling. Often projects involve hundreds of tasks, many of which compete for limited resources, such as certain equipment or skills. Also, some tasks may have to be accomplished during certain time periods or by a certain date. While the manual tracking method suggested by Table 8.2 would not be particularly useful, the linear programming formulation can be adapted for such situations.

Today, however, efficient computer-aided CPM programs are so widely available that it is not worthwhile to extend the linear programming formulation further. Indeed, many of the available programs readily account for seasonal and holiday scheduling, scheduling limited resources, cost–time trade-offs, resource leveling, and sensitivity analyses. Also, computer-aided plotters provide flow diagrams automatically and quickly. Interested readers should inquire about the CPM capabilities available from computer facilities in their area. The main reason for developing this chapter was to provide some insight into the relation of CPM to linear optimization.

CHAPTER 9

SUMMING UP AND CARRYING ON

The thrust of this volume is two-fold! First, that many managerial problems in diverse construction contexts can be formulated as linear optimization problems. Second, that the mathematical and computational technology to solve LP problems is now easy to use, inexpensive, and widely available. This brief Chapter summarizes the basic technical information to here and indicates the character of the ensuing Appendix.

For convenience, the main features of linear optimization problems, noted earlier, are collected here:

1. The general linear programming form (see Chapter 2) is:

   minimize (or maximize):

   $$Z = c_1 X_1 + c_2 X_2 + \cdots + c_n X_n$$

   such that:

   $$a_{11} X_1 + a_{12} X_2 + \cdots + a_{1n} X_n \geq b_1$$
   $$\vdots$$
   $$a_{k1} X_1 + a_{k2} X_2 + \cdots + a_{kn} X_n \leq b_k$$
   $$\vdots$$
   $$a_{m1} X_1 + a_{m2} X_2 + \cdots + a_{mn} X_n = b_m$$

   and

   $$X_1, X_2, \ldots, X_n \geq 0$$

   where $c_1, c_2, \ldots, c_n, a_{11}, a_{12}, \ldots, a_{mn}, b_1, \ldots, b_k, \ldots, b_m$ are constants, and constraints may be of the greater-than, less-than, and/or equality types. In other words, the problem is to determine nonnegative values of the variables $X_1, X_2, \ldots, X_n$ so that Z is an optimum (maximum or minimum) and each of the constraints is satisfied.

2. While the general linear programming form calls for variables that are nonnegative, a simple modification adapts it for variables that may take negative values. (See Section 2.1.)

3. The problem size (number of variables and/or constraints) poses no practical limitation in using linear optimization. (See Section 2.3.)

4. If you can formulate your problem sensibly in a linear optimization format, then you are largely guaranteed that a solution can be obtained routinely and inexpensively by automated computation.

5. Optimal solutions to linear programming problems are global, that is, it is impossible to achieve a better solution in the sense of smaller (or larger) Z with the given information.

6. There may be many solutions having the same optimal value (but not a better one). Multiple solutions enable a manager to choose the one that offers additional advantages such as a shorter duration or uniform workload. (See Section 2.3.)

7. When a job requires decisions that span several time periods, perhaps because the result in one period affects the decision for the next period, time-staged linear programs can be useful. (See Chapter 2, Example 2.)

8. Since numerical data in the linear programming formulation are often "guesstimates," or otherwise subject to uncertainties, it is important to know how sensitive the solution is to the uncertainties. Sensitivity analyses for linear programs are routinely available. (See Section 2.3.)

9. Sometimes variables should have integer values, numbers of trucks, say. Truncating or rounding a noninteger solution is not always satisfactory. Fortunately, many computer programs provide for integer-valued variables in their solution procedures.

Capitalizing on many of these characteristics, we found that many managerial problems in diverse construction contexts could be formulated and solved efficiently as linear optimization problems. The construction management situations included project selection, the basics of critical path methods, construction logistics, blending aggregates, and others. If they are reviewed periodically, useful adaptations for personal situations are likely to come to mind.

The five Appendixes which follow are intended to be integral parts of this book. While some portions may be difficult at first for some readers, they should aid the reader in seeking additional uses of linear optimization in the management of construction.

For example, in steel making, linear optimization is used to determine least-cost monthly plans for the open hearth, production rates of blast furnaces, and the types and quantities of steel scrap to be purchased; while in the lumber industry, linear programming has been used to improve acreage utilization and allocations of timber grades to different finished products. Despite this apparent diversity in use, the linear programs used in these and other industries derive from relatively few prototype models. In Appendix 1 a number of these prototype models are briefly described.

An easily followed description of the basic simplex method of solving linear programs, using "grocery store" arithmetic, is described in Appendix 2. While a computer-aided solution is likely to be most convenient in practical situations, knowing the mechanics of the simplex method is helpful.

The portable (or personal) computer at prices upward from $100 to $150 is now a reality. This means that smaller-sized linear programs can now be solved "in hand." Appendix 3 provides some guidelines.

To help develop skills in formulating linear programs for construction management, a number of problems (some are easy, some are hard) are included in Appendix 4. Some solutions are included for readers who like to compare answers.

Finally, Appendix 5 is a guide to additional reading. References are included for interested readers seeking amplification of points or topics in the main text as well as in the Appendixes.

APPENDIX 1

PROTOTYPE LINEAR OPTIMIZATION MODELS

From the immense variety of applications of linear programming over the years, a relatively small group of basic models (called prototypes) has emerged, which often bear colorful names. While all are mathematically equivalent linear programs, their formats often suggest new applications. For reference, some are outlined here.

A1.1. PRODUCT MIX, FEED MIX, AND GENERAL ALLOCATION PROBLEMS

The simplest linear programming formats are known as the *product mix* and *feed mix* problems.

In the product mix problem, the object is to determine production levels for different products made from (or by) given resources. Usually, each unit yields a given profit, and the objective is to maximize the total profit.

Suppose p_j $(j = 1, \ldots, n)$ is the profit per unit of the jth product, b_i $(i = 1, 2, \ldots, k)$ the available amount of the ith resource, and a_{ij} the amount of the ith resource required to make one unit of the jth product. Then if X_j is the (to be determined) number of units to be made of the jth product, the formulation is:

$$\text{maximize:} \quad Z = p_1 X_1 + p_2 X_2 + \cdots + p_n X_n$$

$$\text{such that:} \quad a_{11} X_1 + a_{12} X_2 + \cdots + a_{1n} X_n \leq b_1$$

$$a_{21} X_1 + a_{22} X_2 + \cdots + a_{2n} X_n \leq b_2$$

$$\vdots$$

$$a_{k1} X_1 + a_{k2} X_2 + \cdots + a_{kn} X_n \leq b_k$$

and $\qquad\qquad X_1, X_2, \ldots, X_n \geq 0$

In a construction context, the "products" might be classes or sizes of jobs to be accomplished, or different materials (say, types of concrete) to be produced. The scarce resources could be man- or machine-hours, or specific types of equipment, materials, or skills.

The feed mix problem is of an opposite type. It requires that product quotas be met at minimum cost. Several production modes, which yield different quantities of each product, are available.

For example, suppose that the required amount (quota) of the ith product is d_i ($i = 1, \ldots, m$), and activity j($j = 1, \ldots, n$), which costs c_j per production run, yields e_{ij} units of the ith product. Then if X_j is the number of times to repeat the jth activity, the problem can be formulated as:

minimize: $\qquad Z = c_1 X_1 + c_2 X_2 + \cdots + c_n X_n$

such that: $\qquad e_{11} X_1 + e_{22} X_2 + \cdots + e_{1n} X_n \geq d_1$

$\qquad\qquad\qquad e_{21} X_1 + e_{22} X_2 + \cdots + e_{2n} X_n \geq d_2$

$$\vdots$$

$\qquad\qquad\qquad e_{m1} X_1 + e_{m2} X_2 + \cdots + e_{mn} X_n \geq d_m$

and $\qquad\qquad X_1, X_2, \ldots, X_n \geq 0$

Recall that this is the form of the quarrying problem of Chapter 1. There the d's represented required amounts of different stone, while X_1 and X_2 were the number of days to operate different quarries. In general, the d_i of the feed mix problem will represent quantities of different materials (concrete, soil, petroleum, and so on) or products (concrete beams, clamps, and so on). The variables X_j could represent any of a number of activities (dredging, quarrying, excavation, fabrication, and so on) at the same or at different locations.

Of course, the distinction between the product mix and the feed mix problems is that in the former (the value of) output is maximized for a given input (that is, resources), while in the latter, (the cost of) input is minimized to achieve a required output (products). Product mix problems inherently assume that all production is useful. In feed mix problems, activities can be undertaken whatever their resource requirements (that is, the resource supply is not limited). Consequently, product mix constraints are all of the less-than type, while feed mix constraints are of the greater-than type.

Often one allocates some scarce (or otherwise valued) resources to meet production quotas. Then constraints of both types, less-than and greater-than, are needed, and perhaps, some equality constraints as well. The objective may be to either minimize cost or maximize profit, depending on the situation. This *general allocation* problem has the format:

minimize: $Z = c_1X_1 + c_2X_2 + \cdots + c_nX_n$

(or maximize: $Z = p_1X_1 + p_2X_2 + \cdots + p_nX_n$)

such that: $a_{11}X_1 + a_{12}X_2 + \cdots + a_{1n}X_n \leq b_1$

$$\vdots$$

$a_{k1}X_1 + a_{k2}X_2 + \cdots + a_{kn}X_n \leq b_k$

$e_{11}X_1 + e_{12}X_2 + \cdots + e_{1n}X_n \geq d_1$

$$\vdots$$

$e_{m1}X_1 + e_{m2}X_2 + \cdots + e_{mn}X_n \geq d_m$

and $X_1, X_2, \cdots, X_n \geq 0$

where a_{ij}, b_i, c_j, d_i, e_{ij}, and p_j are as previously defined. The general allocation problem can be regarded as a combination of the product mix and feed mix problems. More precisely, the latter two are special cases of the former.

A1.2. FLUID BLENDING PROBLEM

The *fluid blending* problem is a variant of the general allocation problem. Again, limited resources are to be allocated among activities to attain quotas for such products as molten metals, crude oils, or other chemical fluids. In addition to the less-than and greater-than constraints (which limit resources and ensure minimum production levels, respectively), certain blending constraints ensure proper ingredient quantities in each product (or mixture).

To illustrate, suppose that a specification requires that the proportion of ingredient i in product j be at least l_{ij}, but not exceed u_{ij} ($l_{ij} < u_{ij}$). If X_{ij} denotes the amount of ingredient i ($i = 1, \ldots, m$) to be included in the jth product, the blending constraint would be written:

$$l_{ij} \leq \frac{X_{ij}}{X_{1j} + X_{2j} + \cdots + X_{mj}} \leq u_{ij}$$

The sum in the denominator is the total amount of the jth product (or blend).

As in the aggregate blending examples of Chapter 3, this blending constraint is actually two linear constraints, that is, first

$$l_{ij} \leq \frac{X_{ij}}{X_{1j} + \cdots + X_{mj}}$$

which can be rewritten as:

$$l_{ij}X_{1j} + l_{ij}X_{2j} + \cdots + (l_{ij} - 1)X_{ij} + \cdots + l_{ij}X_{mj} \leq 0$$

and, second,

$$\frac{X_{ij}}{X_{1j} + \cdots + X_{mj}} \le u_{ij}$$

or, equivalently,

$$u_{ij}X_{1j} + u_{ij}X_{2j} + \cdots + (u_{ij} - 1)X_{ij} + \cdots + u_{ij}X_{mj} \ge 0$$

In this form it is clear that the pair or pairs of blending constraints are identical to the less-than and greater-than constraints of the general allocation problem.

A1.3. TRANSPORTATION PROBLEM

A certain product is stockpiled at several supply centers, and quantities are required at different job sites. The unit cost of shipping the product from each supply center to each job site is given. What quantities should be moved from each center and to which job sites, so that total shipping costs are minimized? This is known as the *transportation* problem.

With some simple assumptions, this common situation can be formulated as a linear optimization problem. Suppose that $b_1, b_2, \ldots, b_m$ are the stored amounts at the m supply centers, and that $d_1, d_2, \ldots, d_n$ are the required quantities at the n job sites. Let X_{ij} be the (unknown) quantity of product to ship from center i to job site j. Then if c_{ij} is the unit cost of shipment, the minimized total cost objective is:

$$
\begin{aligned}
\text{minimize:} \quad Z = \quad & c_{11}X_{11} + c_{12}X_{12} + \cdots + c_{1n}X_n \\
+ \; & c_{21}X_{21} + c_{22}X_{22} + \cdots + c_{2n}X_{2n} \\
& \qquad\qquad\qquad \vdots \\
+ \; & c_{m1}X_{m1} + c_{m2}X_{m2} + \cdots + c_{mn}X_{mn}
\end{aligned}
$$

The constraints form two sets. One set ensures that the quantity shipped from any center does not exceed the amount in storage, that is:

$$X_{11} + X_{12} + \cdots + X_{1n} \le b_1$$
$$X_{21} + X_{22} + \cdots + X_{2n} \le b_2$$
$$\vdots$$
$$X_{m1} + X_{m2} + \cdots + X_{mn} \le b_m$$

The other set ensures that job site requirements are met, that is:

$$X_{11} + X_{21} + \cdots + X_{m1} \ge d_1$$
$$X_{12} + X_{22} + \cdots + X_{m2} \ge d_2$$
$$\vdots$$
$$X_{1n} + X_{2n} + \cdots + X_{mn} \ge d_n$$

Of course, there is the obvious restriction that each $X_{ij} \ge 0$.

Both the objective and the constraint sets can be written more succinctly as:

minimize:
$$Z = \sum_{i=1}^{m} \sum_{j=1}^{n} c_{ij} X_{ij}$$

such that:
$$\sum_{j=1}^{n} X_{ij} \le b_i \quad \text{for } i = 1, 2, \ldots, m$$

$$\sum_{i=1}^{m} X_{ij} \ge d_j \quad \text{for } j = 1, 2, \ldots, n$$

and
$$\text{all } X_{ij} \ge 0$$

Indeed, the earthmoving examples of Chapter 4 and 5 are extensions of the transportation problem. Other construction applications might involve materials, labor, or machinery. The sources or supply centers might be plants, warehouses, storage sites, quarries, or union halls, while the destinations could be construction sites, regional offices, landfills, and so forth. Costs can usually be expressed in dollar units, although units of time or distance may be appropriate.

An interesting aspect of the solution to the transportation problem is that if the requirements (d_j) and the quantities of supply (b_i) are integer-valued, the optimal values of the decision variables will be integers.

A1.4. THE TRANS-SHIPMENT PROBLEM

An extension of the transportation problem is the *trans-shipment* problem, where each destination (and supply center) can act as a point of trans-shipment. Practically speaking, materials can flow into and out of points of trans-shipment depending upon where they are needed most.

As an example, a firm stockpiles a certain product at several locations to be distributed to several job sites. Figure A1.1 illustrates a situation with three supply locations (nodes 1, 3, and 5) and four job sites (nodes 2, 4, 6, and 7). A positive value beside a node indicates the available quantity at that (supply) location, while a negative number indicates the

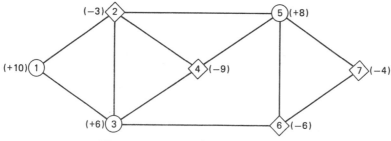

Figure A1.1. Trans-shipment diagram.

quantity required at that job site. The links between nodes might represent highways, rail systems, pipelines, and so forth. The problem is to determine what quantities of materials should be shipped along which routes to meet job site requirements at minimum cost.

Let X_{ij} be the quantity of material shipped between locations (and/or sites) i and j. If c_{ij} is the unit cost of shipping over that link, then the objective is:

$$
\begin{aligned}
\text{minimize:} \quad Z = {} & c_{12}X_{12} + c_{13}X_{13} + c_{21}X_{21} + c_{23}X_{23} \\
& + c_{24}X_{24} + c_{25}X_{25} + c_{31}X_{31} + c_{32}X_{32} + c_{34}X_{34} \\
& + c_{36}X_{36} + c_{42}X_{42} + c_{43}X_{43} + c_{45}X_{45} \\
& + c_{52}X_{52} + c_{54}X_{54} + c_{56}X_{56} + c_{57}X_{57} \\
& + c_{63}X_{63} + c_{65}X_{65} + c_{67}X_{67} + c_{75}X_{75} + c_{76}X_{76}
\end{aligned}
$$

or, more succinctly,

$$
\text{minimize:} \qquad Z = \sum_{i,j} c_{ij}X_{ij}
$$

where the summation is understood to include all possible node connections. Note that for each X_{ij} there is a corresponding X_{ji}. This means that shipment direction is not specified (although, in practical cases, it may be). Of course, X_{ij} and X_{ji} will not both be positive in an optimal solution.

For node 1, the difference between outputs (X_{12} and X_{13}) and inputs (X_{21} and X_{31}) cannot exceed the available quantity (10). Therefore, a constraint is formulated as:

$$
X_{12} + X_{13} - X_{21} - X_{31} \le 10
$$

For node 2, the difference between inputs and outputs must be at least 3, since 3 units of material are required. Therefore, a constraint can be written:

$$
X_{12} + X_{32} + X_{42} + X_{52} - X_{21} - X_{23} - X_{24} - X_{25} \ge 3
$$

and so on for each location.

Capacity constraints may be appropriate over each link, that is:

$$
X_{ij} + X_{ji} \le L_{ij}
$$

where L_{ij} ($= L_{ji}$) is the flow capacity between locations i and j. Both X_{ij} and X_{ji} were included in this sum since the direction of flow is not known as yet.

Finally, a location may have a limited capacity to process (transship) material. For example, if node 2's capacity to receive is limited to R_2, then:

$$
X_{12} + X_{32} + X_{42} + X_{52} \le R_2
$$

A1.5. ASSIGNMENT PROBLEM

Suppose that n tasks can be accomplished by any of n crews (subcontractors, machines, personnel, and so forth). How should assignments, one crew to one task, be made to maximize some measure of value or efficiency (or minimize costs)?

Let v_{ij} be the value of assigning crew i to job j. Then if X_{ij} is defined as a zero–one variable that equals unity if crew i is assigned to job j, and zero otherwise, the problem could be formulated as:

maximize:
$$Z = \sum_{i=1}^{n} \sum_{j=1}^{n} v_{ij} X_{ij}$$

such that:
$$\sum_{j=1}^{n} X_{ij} \leq 1 \qquad \text{each } i = 1, 2, \ldots, n$$

$$\sum_{i=1}^{n} X_{ij} \geq 1 \qquad \text{each } j = 1, 2, \ldots, n$$

and
$$X_{ij} = 0 \quad \text{or} \quad 1, \qquad \text{all } i \text{ and } j$$

The first constraint set ensures that each crew is assigned to (at most) one job; the second set ensures that a crew is assigned to every job; and the third ensures the zero–one character of each variable.

The *assignment* problem suggested here is a special case of the transportation problem when $m = n$, and $b_i = d_j = 1$ for all i and j. The optimal values of the decision variables will always be integer-values and, in this case, equal to zero or one. Therefore, for a computer-aided solution, the integer restrictions are not needed.

A1.6 THE KNAPSACK PROBLEM

Supplies are needed at a remote construction site and there is a limitation on, say, the total weight that can be carried. If each type of supply has a certain utility (that is, a desirability or value), how can the total utility of the cargo be maximized?

Let X_j be the number of units of the jth item to carry, and u_j and w_j the utility and weight of the jth item, respectively.

The objective equation is to maximize the total utility of the cargo, that is:

maximize:
$$Z = \sum_{j=1}^{n} u_j X_j$$

such that the capacity constraint

$$\sum_{j=1}^{n} w_j X_j \leq W$$

is not violated. Here W is the total weight that can be carried and, of course, X_j must be ≥ 0 and integer-valued. Additional constraints to limit the total volume of items carried, or to reflect the need for required (minimum or maximum) quantities of certain items, would be of usual form.

The capital budgeting examples of Chapter 6 are an extension of this *knapsack* problem. There p_j (or u_j) was the profitability of the *j*th type job or contract, b_j (or w_j) was the required investment for that job, and B (or W) represented the total investment potential of the firm. Additional constraints restricted the number of opportunities (that is, the sum of the X_i must be less than some number K_i), and considered limits on available resources (such as supervisory personnel or specific equipment).

A1.7. THE TRIM-LOSS PROBLEM

How should standard lengths of board be cut to meet requirements for shorter lengths if waste is to be minimized?

For example, a contractor has a need for 50 five-foot lengths, 35 nine-foot lengths and 24 eleven-foot lengths of 2×4 lumber. The stock length is 24 feet.

The contractor can cut the 24-foot lengths into any of the following lots (each of which wastes less than 5 feet):

	Board Sizes (numbers of each)			Waste
Lot	5 feet	9 feet	11 feet	(feet)
1	4	0	0	4
2	3	1	0	0
3	2	0	1	3
4	1	2	0	1
5	0	1	1	4
6	0	0	2	2

Other combinations such as $(3,0,0)$, $(1,0,1)$, or $(0,2,0)$ could be used, but they yield less of the required boards than (at least one of) the combinations listed. Therefore, they are excluded.

Let X_i be the number of times to repeat combination i, and let w_i be the trim waste of that combination. Then if a_{ij} is the number of boards of length l_j available using the *i*th combination and b_j is the number required, the linear program (for the general case) is written:

$$\text{minimize:} \qquad \sum_{i=1}^{n} w_i X_i + \sum_{i=1}^{n}\sum_{j=1}^{m} l_j(a_{ij}X_i - b_j)$$

such that:
$$\sum_{i=1}^{n} a_{ij}X_i \geq b_j, \qquad j = 1, \ldots, m$$

and $X_i \geq 0$ and integer.

The first sum in the objective term is clearly the waste (or trim) to be discarded. The second term represents the summation of board lengths produced above the required amounts. Since extra boards are not required, they are considered here as waste although, in practice, they would be retained as substitutes. Interestingly enough, it can be shown that an identical optimal solution (for the value of the X_i) will be obtained if the objective is rewritten as:

minimize:
$$\sum_{i=1}^{n} X_i$$

that is, minimize the number of standard length boards used (cutup).

This *trim-loss* formulation has other applications involving standard lengths of logs, pipes, rebar, rolled shapes, and so on. Problem 23 of Appendix 4 asks the reader to solve the above contractor's problem.

A1.8. THE EMPLOYMENT SCHEDULING AND EQUIPMENT REPLACEMENT PROBLEMS

A firm employs skilled labor at a remote site. There are per diem costs and one-time (setup) costs of orientation, training, and transportation to and from the site. The firm has estimated the number of personnel required daily for the duration of the job (n days). However, requirements fluctuate and workers are hired for varying times. How should the work force be scheduled to minimize total labor cost?

Let X_{ij} be the number of workers who begin work on day i and work through day j, $1 \leq i \leq j \leq n$, and c_{ij} the total employment cost for each such worker. Then the objective equation is written

minimize:
$$Z = \sum_{i=1}^{n} \sum_{j=i}^{n} c_{ij} X_{ij}$$

When N_k workers are required on the kth day, the constraints can be written:

$$\sum_{i=1}^{k} \sum_{j=k}^{n} X_{ij} \geq N_k, \qquad k = 1, 2, \ldots, n$$

and $X_{ij} \geq 0$ and integer for all i and j ($\geq i$).

It is clear why this problem is known as the *employment scheduling* problem. As for the transportation problem, the optimal values of the decision variables X_{ij} will always be integer if the daily requirements N_k are integer.

The *equipment replacement* problem is a related problem. As an example, a firm desires an optimal replacement policy for a machine over an n-year (or period) planning horizon.

Define X_{ij} as a zero–one variable that equals unity if the equipment is purchased in year i and used through year j ($\geq i$), and zero otherwise. Denote by c_{ij} the estimated purchase cost of the equipment in year i, plus its total projected operating and maintenance cost from year i through year j, minus its salvage value at the end of year j. Then the problem can be formulated as:

minimize:
$$Z = \sum_{i=1}^{n} \sum_{j=i}^{n} c_{ij} X_{ij}$$

such that:
$$\sum_{i=1}^{k} \sum_{j=k}^{n} X_{ij} \geq 1, \qquad k = 1, 2, \ldots, n$$

and
$$X_{ij} = 0 \quad \text{or} \quad 1$$

This is identical to the employment scheduling problem formulation when $N_k = 1$, for all k.

It is possible to adapt the formulation to include opportunities for leasing. Let Y_k be a zero–one variable that equals unity if the equipment is leased during year k, and zero if it is not. Let c_k be the lease cost plus the anticipated operation and maintenance cost for year k. Then the formulation becomes:

minimize:
$$Z = \sum_{i=1}^{n} \sum_{j=i}^{n} c_{ij} X_{ij} + \sum_{k=1}^{n} c_k Y_k$$

such that:
$$\sum_{i=1}^{k} \sum_{j=k}^{n} X_{ij} + Y_k \geq 1, \qquad k = 1, \ldots, n$$

and
$$X_{ij}, Y_k = 0 \quad \text{or} \quad 1$$

A1.9 THE WAREHOUSE PROBLEM

Suppose a firm uses a product, say steel beams, over the duration of a job (n periods). The required quantities and the purchase price vary from period to period but can be estimated. If the firm purchases beams for later use, it must pay a storage (or holding) fee per period stored for each beam. How should purchases be scheduled to minimize total cost?

Let X_{ij} be the number of beams purchased in period i for use in period j, $1 \leq i \leq j \leq n$. Let c_{ij} be the total cost (purchase price plus storage costs) of a beam purchased in period i and stored until period j. Then the objective equation is written:

minimize:
$$Z = \sum_{i=1}^{n} \sum_{j=i}^{n} c_{ij} X_{ij}$$

If N_k beams are required in period k, the constraints can be written:

$$\sum_{i=1}^{k} X_{ik} = N_k, \qquad k = 1, 2, \ldots, n$$

and

$$X_{ik} \geq 0 \text{ and integer}$$

This model is known as the *warehouse* problem. Like the related equipment replacement and employment scheduling problems, the optimal values of the decision variables will be integer if the N_k are integer.

Additional constraints are required when the storage capacity is limited, that is:

$$\sum_{i=1}^{k} \sum_{j=i}^{n} X_{ij} - \sum_{i=1}^{k} N_i \leq S_k, \qquad k = 1, \ldots, n-1$$

where S_k is the storage capacity between periods k and $k+1$. The left-hand sides of these constraints represent the difference between the total number of beams purchased and those used through period k. Therefore, this difference equals the number of beams that must be stored between periods k and $k+1$.

In an alternate formulation of the warehouse problem, let c_k be the purchase price in period k $(k = 1, \ldots, n)$, s_k the unit storage price (per beam) between periods k and $k+1$ $(k = 1, \ldots, n-1)$, and N_k the required quantity for period k. Let X_k be the purchase quantity in period k, and Y_k the number of beams to be stored between periods k and $k+1$. Then the objective equation is simply:

minimize: $$Z = \sum_{k=1}^{n} c_k X_k + \sum_{k=0}^{n-1} s_k Y_k$$

It is understood that $Y_0 = 0$ when there are no beams in storage at the beginning of the job (although this need not be the case).

For the constraints:

$$Y_k = Y_{k-1} + X_k - N_k, \qquad k = 1, 2, \ldots, n$$

that is, the amount in storage at the end of any period equals the amount in storage at the beginning of the period plus the amount purchased minus the amount used (required) during that period. These equations can be written equivalently as:

$$X_k + Y_{k-1} - Y_k = N_k, \qquad k = 1, 2, \ldots, n$$

where, again, $Y_0 = 0$.

Additional constraints are required to ensure that the necessary quantities of beams are available, that is:

$$X_k + Y_{k-1} \geq N_k, \qquad k = 1, \ldots, n$$

and, when storage capacity S_k between periods k and $k + 1$ is limiting,

$$Y_k \leq S_k, \qquad k = 1, 2, \ldots, n - 1$$

Of course, both formulations give identical solutions since they represent the same problem. The latter formulation includes n additional (equality) constraints. However, since it has many fewer variables, it will usually be less costly to solve.

The foregoing prototypes are among the better known ones, but they are not exhaustive. The references in Appendix 5 provide guidelines for both intensive and extensive additional readings.

THE SIMPLEX METHOD STEP BY STEP

The *simplex method* is an iterative numerical procedure for solving linear optimization problems. It requires no mathematics beyond "grocery store" arithmetic and, at least in principle, can be used to solve any linear programming problem. The procedure described here requires that the linear programming problem format have these characteristics:

1. The objective equation is to be maximized.
2. All constraints are equations (that is, of the equality type).
3. The constants on the right-hand side of each equation are not negative.
4. All variables may take only nonnegative values.
5. Each constraint has a variable with a positive unit coefficient that does not appear in any other constraint or in the objective equation.

Later we will show that every linear programming problem, whatever its original format, can be modified so that is has these five characteristics.

A2.1.   FUNDAMENTALS OF THE SIMPLEX METHOD

Consider the example problem:

maximize:
$$Z = 5X_1 - 2X_2$$

such that:
$$2X_1 + X_2 + X_3 \qquad\qquad = 9$$
$$X_1 - 2X_2 \qquad + X_4 \qquad = 2$$
$$-3X_1 + 2X_2 \qquad\qquad + X_5 = 3$$

and
$$X_1, X_2, \ldots, X_5 \geq 0$$

Clearly, it has all of the above five characteristics: the problem requires a maximization, all three constraints are equations with nonnegative constants on the right-hand side, all variables are indicated to be non-negative, and each constraint has one variable (either X_3, X_4, or X_5) that appears only in itself and with a unit coefficient. It is customary to refer to variables that satisfy the fifth characteristic as *basic variables,* and to those that do not (that is, all others) as *nonbasic variables.*

To aid in explaining and applying the simplex method, it is helpful to rewrite the above problem into the following tabular format:

Row	Z	X_1	X_2	X_3	X_4	X_5	RHS
0	1	-5	$+2$				0
1		2	1	1			9
2		1	-2		1		2
3		-3	2			1	3

This *simplex tableau* shows each coefficient of the problem in its corresponding row and beneath its respective variable. For later reference, the basic variables X_3, X_4, and X_5 (as well as the objective Z) have been indicated in boldface type. The constants in the right-hand column are, of course, the values on the right-hand sides of the constraint equations. Note that the objective function has been represented as:

$$Z - 5X_1 + 2X_2 = 0$$

which is equivalent to the original objective $Z = 5X_1 - 2X_2$. The absence of an entry in any row (or column) of the simplex tableau should be considered as (an unwritten) zero.

Using this tableau, we describe the step-by-step simplex procedure.

STEP 1.   First, select a negative coefficient in the zero (objective) row of the tableau. For clarity, place a box around it.

For example, there is only one negative objective row coefficient (-5) in the above tableau, so it is boxed, that is:

Row	Z	X_1	X_2	X_3	X_4	X_5	RHS
0	1	$\boxed{-5}$	2				0
1		2	1	1			9
2		1	-2		1		2
3		-3	2			1	3

When there are two or more negative coefficients in the 0 row, as a rule of thumb, select the smallest (i.e., most negative); for example, choose -10 before -5. In case of a tie, select either.

STEP 2. Divide each positive entry below the boxed coefficient selected in step 1 into the corresponding constant in the right-hand column. Circle the positive entry for the smallest ratio.

For example, there are two positive entries in the X_1 column, corresponding to rows (or constraints) 1 and 2. The ratios are 9/2 and 2/1, respectively. Therefore, the unit coefficient under X_1 is circled.

Row	Z	X_1	X_2	X_3	X_4	X_5	RHS	
0	1	$\boxed{-5}$	2				0	
1		2	1	1			9	(9/2 = 4.5)
2		①	-2		1		2	(2/1 = 2)
3		-3	2			1	3	—

The circled entry is called a *pivot element,* and its row, the *pivot row.* Had there been a tie for the smallest ratio, either of the corresponding entries could be chosen (circled) as the pivot element.

If all entries under a negative objective row coefficient are either negative or zero, then the maximum value of Z is $+\infty$. Since this could not be the answer to any practical problem, probably one or more constraints were neglected in the formulation, or perhaps an error was made in transcription or arithmetic. The cause must be found and remedied before the simplex method can continue.

STEP 3. Divide all entries in the pivot row (including the constant in the right column) by the value of the pivot element. Record the resulting numbers in a new tableau.

Here the pivot row (constraint 2) is copied directly because the pivot element equals unity:

Row	Z	X_1	X_2	X_3	X_4	X_5	RHS
0							
1							
2		1	-2		1		2
3							

STEP 4.   Eliminate all other entries in the column selected in step 1 by adding (or subtracting) suitable multiples of the new pivot row to (or from) each row in the preceding (complete) tableau. Record the results in the new tableau.

Here the entries in the new pivot row (row 2) are first multiplied by $+5$, which yields 0, 5, -10, 0, 5, 0, and 10. (Remember, blank entries in the tableau are actually zeros.) These numbers are then added column by column to the entries of row 0 (objective). The result is recorded in the new tableau:

Row	Z	X_1	X_2	X_3	X_4	X_5	RHS
0	1		-8		5		10
1							
2		1	-2		1		2
3							

To complete this tableau, the pivot row entries are now multiplied by 2 and subtracted from the row 1 entries, and then multiplied by 3 and added to the row 3 entries.

The resulting complete tableau is:

Row	Z	$\mathbf{X_1}$	X_2	$\mathbf{X_3}$	X_4	$\mathbf{X_5}$	RHS
0	1		-8		5		10
1			5	1	-2		5
2		1	-2		1		2
3			-4		3	1	9

Note that each constraint still has the required fifth characteristic, that is, each has a basic variable that appears nowhere else in the tableau, with a unit coefficient. This should always be the case if the arithmetic operations are performed correctly. In this case the basic variables are $\mathbf{X_1}$, $\mathbf{X_3}$, and $\mathbf{X_5}$, as indicated by boldface type.

STEP 5.   Repeat steps 1 through 4 until there are no negative coefficients in row 0 (objective).

There was still a negative entry (-8 under X_2) in row 0 of the last tableau. Since there is only one positive entry ($+5$) in the corresponding column, it must be the pivot element. All entries in the pivot row (row 1) are divided by 5 and entered in the new tableau:

Row	Z	X_1	X_2	X_3	X_4	X_5	RHS
0							
1			1	1/5	-2/5		1
2							
3							

Finally, repeating step 4 yields:

Row	Z	X_1	X_2	X_3	X_4	X_5	RHS
0	1			8/5	9/5		18
1			1	1/5	-2/5		1
2		1		2/5	1/5		4
3				4/5	7/5	1	13

There are no negative coefficients in row 0 (objective) of this tableau. Therefore, the optimal solution is at hand.

STEP 6.   The maximum value of Z, that is Z^*, appears as the extreme upper right entry in the final tableau. The optimal value of each basic variable appears in the right-hand column of the row corresponding to its unit coefficient. All other variables are nonbasic and equal zero.

The optimal solution for the previous problem can be read directly from the final tableau, that is:

$$Z^* = 18$$

and

$$X_1 = 4, \qquad X_2 = 1, \qquad X_5 = 13$$

The nonbasic variables X_3 and X_4 equal zero. As a check, these values can be substituted in the original constraint equations to see that each is satisfied. Also, substitution in the original objective function yields $Z = 18$.

STEP 7.   If a coefficient of a nonbasic variable in row 0 (objective) equals zero, multiple optima exist. To obtain other optimal solutions, box the zero coefficient and repeat steps 2 through 6.

For example, suppose that the original problem had as its objective:

maximize: $Z = 5X_1 - 10X_2$

along with the original constraints. The initial tableau would be:

Row	Z	X_1	X_2	X_3	X_4	X_5	RHS
0	1	-5	$+10$				0
1		2	1	1			9
2		1	-2		1		2
3		-3	2			1	3

and the first new tableau is:

Row	Z	X_1	X_2	X_3	X_4	X_5	RHS
0	1				5		10
1			5	1	-2		5
2		1	-2		1		2
3			-4		3	1	9

Since there are no negative coefficients in row 0 of this last tableau, the optimal solution has been obtained. In this case,

$$Z^* = 10$$

and

$$X_1 = 2, \qquad X_3 = 5, \qquad X_5 = 9$$

and the nonbasic variables X_2 and X_4 equal zero. However, X_2 has a zero coefficient in row 0 (objective). This is an unfailing signal that the problem has multiple optima.

To obtain another optimal solution, box the (unwritten) zero directly under X_2. Select $+5$ as the pivot element since it is the only positive entry in that column, and following steps 3 and 4, form the new tableau:

Row	Z	X_1	X_2	X_3	X_4	X_5	RHS
0	1				9/5		10
1			1	1/5	$-2/5$		1
2		1		2/5	1/5		4
3				4/5	7/5	1	13

Here an alternative optimal solution is given as:

$$Z^* = 10$$

and

$$X_1 = 4, \qquad X_2 = 1, \qquad X_5 = 13$$

and $X_3 = X_4 = 0$. Of course, the value of Z^* remains unchanged. This time X_3 is a nonbasic variable with a zero-valued objective row coefficient. In this case, if step 7 is repeated a second time, the previous solution will be obtained.

If there were two or more nonbasic variables with zero-valued objective row coefficients, additional alternative optima could be found by boxing a different zero coefficient and applying the procedure again.

As indicated in Chapter 2, every point on a line segment joining alternative optima is also an optimum. These solutions can be obtained from the formula:

$$X_j^{(w)} = (1 - w)X_j^{(0)} + wX_j^{(1)}, \qquad 0 \le w \le 1$$

where $X_j^{(0)}$ and $X_j^{(1)}$ are values for X_j in two optimal solutions (the superscripts are used only to distinguish among the two solutions), and w is any number between 0 and 1 inclusive. The formula must be applied to each variable in the problem.

For example, the two optimal solutions in the previous tableaux were:

$$X_1^{(0)} = 2, \qquad X_1^{(1)} = 4$$
$$X_2^{(0)} = 0, \qquad X_2^{(1)} = 1$$
$$X_3^{(0)} = 5, \qquad X_3^{(1)} = 0$$
$$X_4^{(0)} = 0, \qquad X_4^{(1)} = 0$$
$$X_5^{(0)} = 9, \qquad X_5^{(1)} = 13$$
$$Z^* = 10$$

Therefore, the values of additional solutions can be determined from the equations:

$$X_1^{(w)} = (1 - w) \times X_1^{(0)} + w \times X_1^{(1)}$$
$$(1 - w) \times 2 \quad + w \times 4 = 2(1 + w)$$
$$X_2^{(w)} = (1 - w) \times 0 \quad + w \times 1 = w$$
$$X_3^{(w)} = (1 - w) \times 5 \quad + w \times 0 = 5(1 - w)$$
$$X_4^{(w)} = (1 - w) \times 0 \quad + w \times 0 = 0$$
$$X_5^{(w)} = (1 - w) \times 9 \quad + w \times 13 = 9 + 4w$$

Choosing w arbitrarily, say $w = 1/2$, yields the optimal values:

$$X_1 = 3, \qquad X_2 = 1/2, \qquad X_3 = 5/2, \qquad X_4 = 0, \qquad X_5 = 11$$

and

$$Z^* = 5X_1 - 10X_2 = 15 - 5 = 10$$

as expected.

A2.2.   OBTAINING THE FIVE REQUIRED CHARACTERISTICS

Virtually every linear program can be transformed into a form with the five characteristics cited at the outset. Let us see how.

Minimization

Minimization of any objective equation is equivalent to maximizing its negative, subject to the same constraints. Therefore, to change a minimization problem to one of maximization, simply change the sign of each objective coefficient. The solution value for the objective of the maximization problem will just be the negative of the optimal value for the original (minimization) problem.

For example, if a linear programming problem requires minimization of $Z = 5X_1 - 2X_2$, simply replace the objective equation by:

$$Z' = (-Z) = -5X_1 + 2X_2$$

and maximize. If the solution to the maximization problem is $Z' = +3$, the minimum value of the original problem is $Z = -3$.

Inequalities

To change an inequality constraint to an equation (equality), simply add a new nonnegative variable on the lesser side, and replace the inequality sign by an equality.

For a less-than constraint, say,

$$2X_1 + X_2 \leq 9$$

introduce a new nonnegative variable (call it X_s) on the left-hand side and write:

$$2X_1 + X_2 + X_s = 9$$

Because it supplies the slack in the original constraint, X_s is appropriately called a *slack variable*.

For a greater-than constraint, say,

$$2X_1 + X_2 \geq 4$$

simply add a new nonnegative variable (call it X_e) on the right-hand side and write:

$$2X_1 + X_2 = 4 + X_e$$

or, equivalently,

$$2X_1 + X_2 - X_e = 4$$

The latter form is necessary for the simplex method. Here, since X_e is subtracted from the original variable terms, it is frequently called an *excess variable*.

Negative right-hand sides

If after changing all constraints to equalities, any constraint has a negative constant on its right-hand side, change the signs of all its terms.
    Consider the equality constraint:

$$3X_1 - 2X_2 - X_e = -3$$

This constraint can be written equivalently as:

$$-3X_1 + 2X_2 + X_e = 3$$

Variables unrestricted in sign

A variable whose values could be negative must be replaced by the difference of two nonnegative variables.
    For example, suppose that the variable X_1 in the earlier problem could meaningfully be negative as well as positive. It should be replaced by the difference of two new nonnegative variables, say,

$$X_1 = X_6 - X_7$$

The modified formulation would be:

maximize: $Z = 5(X_6 - X_7) - 2X_2$

such that: $2(X_6 - X_7) + X_2 + X_3 = 9$

$(X_6 - X_7) - 2X_2 + X_4 = 2$

$-3(X_6 - X_7) + 2X_2 + X_5 = 3$

and $X_2, X_3, \ldots, X_6, X_7 \geq 0$

Constraints without basic variables

Add a new nonnegative variable to the left-hand side of each constraint that lacks the fifth characteristic. Also, subtract this same variable, multiplied by a very large (but arbitrary) positive number, from the (maximization) objective equation. Then form the simplex tableau and apply step 4 of the simplex method (repeating as necessary) to remove this new variable term from row 0 (objective).

Such variables, added to an (already) equality, are referred to as *artificial variables*. Clearly, they must take the value zero (in the final solution) if the equal sign is to hold. This is the reason a large multiple of each artifical variable is subtracted from the objective equation. Since the simplex method attempts to maximize, it will choose values of the artificial variables as small as possible, that is, equal to zero, since they must be nonnegative. If any of the artificial variables are other than zero in the final solution, either an error was made in arithmetic, the (arbitrary) multiple was not large enough, or the original problem does not have a finite optimum.

This scheme seems difficult to follow at first, and an example is helpful. Suppose that a linear programming problem has been formulated as:

minimize: $\qquad\qquad\qquad\quad Z = 3X_1 + 2X_2$

such that: $\qquad\qquad\qquad\ 3X_1 + X_2 = 12$

$$X_1 \qquad\ \geq\ 3$$

$$X_2 \geq -4$$

where $X_1 \geq 0$ but X_2 is unrestrained in sign. To transform it to the required format, first change the objective to maximization by changing the signs of each coefficient, that is, rewrite the objective as:

maximize:

$$Z' = (-Z) = -3X_1 - 2X_2$$

Since both the second and the third constraints are greater-than inequalities, add an excess variable to the right-hand side of each constraint, or, equivalently, subtract excess variables from the left-hand side. Then change the inequality signs to equalities. For example, if the excess variables are X_{e2} and X_{e3}, these two constraints can be rewritten as:

$$X_1\ -\ X_{e2}\qquad\quad =\ 3$$

$$X_2 \qquad -\ X_{e3} = -4$$

Next, the coefficients of this last equality constraint are changed so that the right-hand side is positive. That is,

$$-X_2 \qquad\quad +\ X_{e3} =\ 4$$

Since X_2 can be negative or positive, it is replaced by the difference of two new variables, say X_3 and X_4. Substituting $X_2 = X_3 - X_4$ throughout, the problem is reformulated as:

maximize: $\qquad Z' = (-Z) = -3X_1 - 2(X_3 - X_4)$

such that:
$$3X_1 + (X_3 - X_4) \qquad\qquad = 12$$
$$X_1 \qquad\qquad - X_{e2} \qquad = 3$$
$$+ (X_3 - X_4) \qquad + X_{e3} = 4$$

and
$$X_1, X_3, X_4, X_{e2}, X_{e3} \geq 0$$

Expressed in tabular format, the problem is:

Row	Z′	X_1	X_3	X_4	X_{e2}	$\mathbf{X_{e3}}$	RHS
0	1	3	2	-2			0
1		3	1	-1			12
2		1			-1		3
3			-1	1		1	4

Recall that in tabular format the coefficients of the variable terms in the objective function change sign because they are moved to the left-hand side of the equal sign.

In tabular form it is easy to see that X_{e3} is a basic variable for the third constraint, that is, it satisfies the fifth characteristic. However, the first and second constraints lack such variables. Therefore, new artificial variables, say X_{a1} and X_{a2}, are added to the left-hand sides of these constraints. Also, a large multiplier of these variables must be subtracted from the right-hand side of the objective function.

The revised problem in equation form is:

maximize: $Z' = -3X_1 - 2X_3 + 2X_4 - MX_{a1} - MX_{a2}$

such that: $3X_1 + X_3 - X_4 + X_{a1} \qquad\qquad = 12$
$$X_1 \qquad\qquad + X_{a2} - X_{e2} \qquad = 3$$
$$- X_3 + X_4 \qquad\qquad + X_{e3} = 4$$

or in tabular form:

Row	Z′	X_1	X_3	X_4	X_{a1}	X_{a2}	X_{e2}	$\mathbf{X_{e3}}$	RHS
0	1	3	2	-2	$+M$	$+M$			0
1		3	1	-1	1				12
2		1				1	-1		3
3			-1	+1				1	4

where X_1, X_3, X_4, X_{a1}, X_{a2}, X_{e2}, and $X_{e3} \geq 0$, and M is some large positive coefficient.

Suppose that M is chosen to be 50. Using step 4, all entries in constraint 1 are multiplied by (-50) and added to row 0 (objective); likewise for constraint 2. The resulting tableau is:

Row	Z'	X_1	X_3	X_4	X_{a1}	X_{a2}	X_{e2}	X_{e3}	RHS
0	1	-197	-48	48			$+50$		-750
1		3	1	-1	1				12
2		1				1	-1		3
3			-1	1				1	4

Finally the problem is in a form for using the simplex method. Begin (step 1) by boxing the most negative coefficient in row 0, that is, -197 under X_1. There are two positive entries in the X_1 column, and the corresponding ratios (step 2) are $12/3 = 4$ and $3/1 = 3$ for constraints 1 and 2, respectively. Since the latter ratio is smaller, constraint 2 is the pivot row and its X_1 coefficient, the pivot element. Since the pivot element equals unity, row 2 is copied directly into a new tableau (step 3), that is:

Row	Z'	X_1	X_3	X_4	X_{a1}	X_{a2}	X_{e2}	X_{e3}	RHS
0									
1									
2		1				1	-1		3
3									

To remove the X_1 coefficient from row 0 (step 4), each pivot row entry is multiplied by 197 and added to its corresponding objective row entry. Similarly, pivot row entries are multiplied by 3 and subtracted from the row 1 entries to eliminate the X_1 coefficient in that row. Row 3 does not require any modification because its X_1 coefficient is already zero. Entering these results, the new tableau becomes:

Row	Z'	X_1	X_3	X_4	X_{a1}	X_{a2}	X_{e2}	X_{e3}	RHS
0	1		-48	48		197	-147		-159
1			1	-1	1	-3	3		3
2		1				1	-1		3
3			-1	1				1	4

Repeating the procedure for this tableau yields the following:

Row	Z'	X_1	X_3	X_4	X_{a1}	X_{a2}	X_{e2}	X_{e3}	RHS
0	1		1	−1	49	50			−12
1			1/3	−1/3	1/3	−1	1		1
2		1	1/3	−1/3	1/3				4
3			−1	1				1	4

There is still a negative entry in the objective function, so the procedure is not complete. Repeating the simplex method once again, yields the tableau:

Row	Z'	X_1	X_3	X_4	X_{a1}	X_{a2}	X_{e2}	X_{e3}	RHS
0	1				49	50		1	−8
1					1/3	−1	1	1/3	7/3
2		1			1/3			1/3	16/3
3			−1	1				1	4

Since all coefficients in row 0 are positive (or zero), this solution is optimal. Its values are $(Z')^* = -8$ when $X_1 = 16/3$, $X_4 = 4$, $X_{e2} = 7/3$, and all other variables equal zero. Of course, since $X_2 = X_3 - X_4$, its optimal value is:

$$X_2 = 0 - 4 = -4$$

The optimal (minimum) value of the original objective function, that is, $Z^* = -(Z')^* = 8$, is easily verified by substituting the values $X_1 = 16/3$ and $X_2 = -4$ into the original objective equation.

PERSONAL COMPUTERS

Throughout the text the implication has been that solutions to linear programs are readily obtainable at reasonable cost from computing centers (or services) or that smaller-sized linear programs could be solved by hand. Indeed, that has been the experience for the past two decades in which the main text examples evolved. It is now possible to report a substantial new development — the personal or portable computer.

A hand-held computer, capable of being programmed to solve at least smaller linear optimization problems, is now available in the $100 to $200 price range. Useful accessories such as a cassette interface, additional memory, a printer, and/or a TV display can double or triple the outlay. Still, by the standards of just a few years ago, the computing power in a hand-held instrument and for under several hundred dollars is an historic milestone. Some portable computers in this category are the Casio FX702P, the Radio Shack PC1 or PC2, the Sharp PC1500, and the Hewlett-Packard HP-75C.

The linear program computing capability is likely to vary according to the available program, problem, added memory, and perhaps other factors not yet understood. Since well developed software for linear programs on personal computers is not widely available and tested at this writing, it is not possible to provide reliable measures of problem sizes that can be solved by these devices.

Mr. R. N. Pratt, Engineering Computation Specialist at the University of Delaware, has devised first-generation programs in Basic for the Sharp PC1500 and the Casio FX702P. They appear in Displays A3.1 and A3.2, respectively. The Radio Shack PC-2 hand-held computer will also run the Sharp program. At the conclusion of the programs in the two displays appears the solution to this simple problem:

$$\text{maximize:} \qquad Z = 2X_1 - 3X_2 + 3X_3$$

```
5:REM SIMPLEX AL
  GORITHM: SHARP
  PC1500 POCKET
  COMPUTER
7:REM
8:REM INPUT SECT
  ION
9:REM
10:INPUT "NO. OF
  CONSTRAINTS";
  M
20:INPUT "NO. OF
  VARIABLES";N
30:DIM A(M,N)
40:PAUSE "ENTER A
  (I,J).S":WAIT
  0
50:FOR I=1TO M
60:FOR J=1TO N
70:PRINT "A(";I;"
  ,";J;") ";:
  INPUT A(I,J):
  CLS
80:NEXT J:NEXT I
90:DIM B(M)
95:REM B VALUE MU
  ST BE >=0.
96:REM IF NOT, AD
  D EXTRA VARIAB
  LE AND ADJUST
  OBJ FUNCTION.
100:FOR I=1TO M
110:PRINT "B(";I;"
  ) ";:INPUT B(I
  ):CLS
120:NEXT I
130:DIM C(N)
140:FOR J=1TO N
150:PRINT "C(";J;"
  )";:INPUT C(J)
  :CLS
160:NEXT J
195:REM
196:REM COMPUTATIO
  N SECTION
197:REM
200:DIM IT(M):DIM
  JT(N)
210:J=1
220:JT(J)=J
230:IF J-N=0GOTO 2
  60
240:IF J-N>0THEN
  STOP
250:J=J+1:GOTO 220
260:I=1
270:IT(I)=I+N:IF I
  -M=0GOTO 300
280:IF I-M>0THEN
  STOP
```

```
290:I=I+1:GOTO 270
300:J=1
310:IF C(J)>0GOTO
  350
320:IF J-N=0GOTO 7
  20
330:IF J-N>0THEN
  STOP
340:J=J+1:GOTO 310
350:K=J
360:I=1:Q=0:R=1.E6
370:IF A(I,K)>0
  GOTO 410
380:IF I-M=0GOTO 4
  30
390:IF I-M>0THEN
  STOP
400:I=I+1:GOTO 370
410:T=B(I)/A(I,K):
  IF T-R>=0GOTO
  380
420:R=T:Q=I:GOTO 3
  80
430:IF Q<0THEN
  STOP
440:IF Q=0GOTO 990
450:E=IT(Q):IT(Q)=
  JT(K)
460:JT(K)=E
470:A(Q,K)=1/A(Q,K
  ):J=1
480:IF J<>KGOTO 51
  0
490:IF J=NGOTO 520
500:J=J+1:GOTO 480
510:A(Q,J)=A(Q,J)*
  A(Q,K):GOTO 49
  0
520:B(Q)=B(Q)*A(Q,
  K):I=1
530:IF I-Q<>0GOTO
  570
540:IF I-M=0GOTO 6
  50
550:IF I-M>0THEN
  STOP
560:I=I+1:GOTO 530
570:J=1
580:IF J-K=0GOTO 6
  00
590:A(I,J)=A(I,J)-
  A(I,K)*A(Q,J)
600:IF J-N=0GOTO 6
  30
610:IF J-N>0THEN
  STOP
620:J=J+1:GOTO 580
630:B(I)=B(I)-A(I,
  K)*B(Q)
```

```
640:A(I,K)=-A(I,K)
  *A(Q,K):GOTO 5
  40
650:J=1
660:IF J-K=0GOTO 6
  80
670:C(J)=C(J)-C(K)
  *A(Q,J)
680:IF J-N<0GOTO 7
  10
690:IF J-N>0THEN
  STOP
700:C(K)=-C(K)*A(Q
  ,K):GOTO 300
710:J=J+1:GOTO 660
715:REM
716:REM OUTPUT SEC
  TION
717:REM
720:WAIT :FOR I=1
  TO M:PRINT "X(
  ";IT(I);") =";
  B(I):NEXT I:
  END
990:PRINT "UNBOUND
  ED":END
```

```
# CONSTRAINTS    4
# VARIABLES      3
ENTER A(I,J).S
A( 1, 1)    -2
A( 1, 2)     3
A( 1, 3)     0
A( 2, 1)     1
A( 2, 2)    -2
A( 2, 3)    -4
A( 3, 1)     2
A( 3, 2)     1
A( 3, 3)     1
A( 4, 1)     1
A( 4, 2)     1
A( 4, 3)     5
ENTER B(I).S
B( 1)     2
B( 2)     5
B( 3)     6
B( 4)    10
ENTER C(J).S
C( 1)     2
C( 2)    -3
C( 3)     3
X( 4) = 6.444E 00
X( 5) = 8.999E 00
X( 1) = 2.222E 00
X( 3) = 1.555E 00
```

Display A.3.1. Linear optimization program for Sharp PC1500.

LIST #0

```
  1 PRT "CASIO FX70
    2P":PRT "SIMPLE
    X ALGORITHM"
  5 INP "DIMNS",M,N
    :U=M*N:V=U+M:W=
    V+N:X=W+M
 10 WAIT 75:PRT "EN
    TER A(I,J).S"
 20 FOR I=1 TO M:FO
    R J=1 TO N:INP
    A(N*(I-1)+J:NE
    XT J:NEXT I
 30 PRT "ENTER B(I)
    .S, C(J).S"
 40 FOR I=U+1 TO W:
    INP A(I):NEXT I
210 J=1
220 A(J+X)=J
230 IF J-N=0 THEN 2
    60
240 IF J-N>0;STOP
250 J=J+1:GOTO 220
260 I=1
270 A(I+W)=I+N:IF I
    -M=0 THEN 300
280 IF I-M>0;STOP
290 I=I+1:GOTO 270
300 J=1
310 IF A(J+V)>0 THE
    N 350
320 IF J-N=0 THEN 8
    00
330 IF J-N>0 THEN S
    TOP
340 J=J+1:GOTO 310
350 K=J
360 I=1:Q=0:R=1.E6
370 IF A(N*(I-1)+K)
    >0 THEN 410
380 IF I-M=0 THEN 4
    30
390 IF I-M>0;STOP
400 I=I+1:GOTO 370
410 T=A(I+U)/A(N*(I
    -1)+K,:IF T-R≥0
    THEN 380
420 R=T:Q=I:GOTO 38
    0
430 IF Q<0;STOP
440 IF Q=0 THEN 990
450 E=A(W+Q):A(W+Q)
    =A(X+K)
460 A(X+K)=E
470 L=N*(Q-1)+K:A(L
    )=1/A(L):J=1
480 IF J≠K THEN 510
```

```
490 IF J=N THEN 520
500 J=J+1:GOTO 480
510 L=N*(Q-1)+J:A(L
    )=A(L)*A(L-J+K)
    :GOTO 490
520 A(U+Q)=A(U+Q)*A
    (N*(Q-1)+K):I=1
530 IF I-Q≠0 THEN 5
    70
540 IF I-M=0 THEN 6
    50
550 IF I-M>0;STOP
560 I=I+1:GOTO 530
570 J=1
580 IF J-K=0 THEN 6
    00
590 L=N*(I-1)+J:A(L
    )=A(L)-A(L-J+K)
    *A(N*(Q-1)+J)
600 IF J-N=0 THEN 6
    30
610 IF J-N>0;STOP
620 J=J+1:GOTO 580
630 A(I+U)=A(I+U)-A
    (N*(I-1)+K)*A(Q
    +U)
640 L=N*(I-1)+K:A(L
    )=-A(L)*A(N*(Q-
    1)+K):GOTO 540
650 J=1
660 IF J-K=0 THEN 6
    80
670 A(J+V)=A(J+V)-A
    (K+V)*A(N*(Q-1)
    +J)
680 IF J-N<0 THEN 7
    10
690 IF J-N>0;STOP
700 A(V+K)=-A(V+K)*
    A(N*(Q-1)+K):GO
    TO 300
710 J=J+1:GOTO 660
800 FOR I=1 TO M:PR
    T "X(";A(W+I);"
    ) = ";A(U+I):NE
    XT I:STOP
990 PRT "UNBOUNDED"
    :END
```

```
RUN

CASIO FX702P

SIMPLEX ALGORITHM

DIMNS?
4
?
3
ENTER A(I,J).S
?
-2
?
3
?
0
?
1
?
-2
?
-4
?
2
?
1
?
1
?
1
?
1
?
5
ENTER B(I).S, C(J).S
?
2
?
5
?
6
?
10
?
2
?
-3
?
3
X( 4) = 6.444444444
X( 5) = 9
X( 1) = 2.222222222
X( 3) = 1.555555556
```

Display A.3.2. Linear optimization program for Casio FX702P.

such that:
$$-2X_1 + 3X_2 \qquad \leq 2$$
$$X_1 - 2X_2 - 4X_3 \leq 5$$
$$2X_1 + X_2 + X_3 \leq 6$$
$$X_1 + X_2 + 5X_3 \leq 10$$

and
$$X_1, X_2, X_3 \geq 0$$

There is the expectation that software suitable for these and newer generations of personal computers and accessories will soon be available and that the authors and readers will gain experience in their construction management uses. The authors welcome related correspondence to the address at the end of the Preface.

The Preface cautioned against "get rich quick" expectations — and that still holds. A great deal depends upon individual familiarity with the strengths and weaknesses of linear optimization, the nature of one's business, and developing a skill in formulating managerial problems advantageously. There are many and powerful facets to linear programs that could not be included in this volume. This is the case not only because they exceeded the present scope but also because the contents were restricted to applications with which we could claim experience.

Considering that personal computers (to say nothing about main frame terminals) are likely to be office staples for many readers, the marginal cost of solving linear optimization problems is nil. When this prospect is coupled with the many more advanced features of linear optimization that one can learn and the very limited usage of linear programming to date, solving such problems becomes worthy of serious evaluation for every manager of engineered construction.

As noted in the text, most of the displays are outputs of the Burroughs B7700 computer, which was convenient for us. While it has nothing to do with personal computers, this is a convenient place to reprint some information provided by the University of Delaware's Computing Center for users of the software package titled "LP" on the B7700. It should be helpful to further familiarize the reader with the format of the displays in the text.

A3.1. HOW TO USE LP

The commands control various portions of the problem solution process. Thus the LOAD command is used to enter a new problem, the SOLVE command finds the linear solution of the currently loaded problem, and the ALL, STD, and NONE commands control which tableaux are printed during solution.

A prompt of --> indicates that the program is waiting for a command to be entered. When using a punched deck, you anticipate these prompts.

Input lines can be no more than 80 characters long. If an objective function or constraint is longer than 80 characters, then type part of it, type a comma, and press RETURN. The program understands that any line ending with a comma is to be continued and it will prompt with a -->. Following are the basic commands you will need to use LP.

LOAD

Typing LOAD initiates problem loading. The program types OBJ*FN, and you then enter MAXIMIZE or MINIMIZE followed by the objective function in standard algebraic notation. All of the below would be acceptable objective functions:

OBJ*FN MINIMIZE 2X − 3Y + Z
OBJ*FN MAXIMIZE −2X1 + 3X2 − Q
OBJ*FN MIN 2 CHAIRS − 3 TABLES + SETEE

The names you gave to your variables will be used to label the tableaux and the final results generated by the SOLVE command. All names must start with a letter, and if something follows a name, it must be a plus or a minus sign. Names are not required. Multiplication and division are not allowed in either the objective function or the constraints.
IMPORTANT: All variables must appear in the objective function, even those with zero coefficients.

When you type in a viable objective function, the program will respond by typing CON1. This is your cue to enter the first constraint. Each constraint consists of a linear expression, a relational operator, and a right-hand-side value, in that order. The relational operator can be any of the following:

<=   for "less than or equal to"
\>=   for "greater than or equal to"
=   for "equal to"

The coefficients in a constraint need not be named if their order and number agree with the objective function. Spacing is ignored and so can be used to improve readability. Below is a sample problem which illustrates some of the allowable forms:

OBJ*FN MAX 3X + 2Y + 0Z
CON1   6   − 3   + 2 <= 100
CON2   2X + 4.1Y + 3Z = 10.247
CON4   3Z + 2X >= 10
CON5   Z <= 3

To leave the LOAD mode press the RETURN key.

NOTE: An equality constraint generates two constraints internally, and this fact is reflected in the constraint numbering scheme (see CON2 above).

Note also that all variables must be present in the objective function, and new variables cannot be added except during LOAD. Constraints also can only be added or deleted during a LOAD.

SOLVE

Typing SOLVE initiates solution of the currently LOADed problem for a linear result. The solution is printed along with the initial and final tableaux. The tableaux are printed in a modified simplex form wherein slack constraints are removed.

NONE

Causes the SOLVE command to not print any tableaux. Entering ALL will cause all tableaux to be printed, and entering STD causes just the first and last tableaux to be printed.

SENSITIVITY

Causes sensitivity analysis to be done whenever a problem is SOLVEd. Advanced commands tell how to request integer and zero–one solutions to your problem. Sensitivity analysis can be used with these types of solution, but results obtained are not necessarily correct.

Sensitivity analysis is shut off with the NONSENSITIVITY command.

STOP

Stops the program.

APPENDIX 4

PROBLEM SET

PROBLEM 1*

Rollin Along needs these quantities of stone for his next job:

720 tons of Softa stone
600 tons of Harda stone
330 tons of Common stone

New equipment at Quarry 1 has increased output by 25% to 100, 75, and 25 tons of the respective types of stones in a day of operation. The output at Quarry 2, as before, is 40, 80, and 60 tons per day, respectively. How should the single quarry crew be deployed to produce the required stone in the least time?

PROBLEM 2

Use graphical methods to follow up these suggestions relating to the quarrying problem of Chapters 1 and 2.
(a)   Increase the required amount of Softa stone to 500 tons daily. Show that the minimum quarrying time is increased to 7.5 days, as suggested in Section 2.3.
(b)   The 180 tons of Common stone are no longer needed. How does the removal of this requirement for stone alter the solution? Also, suppose an alternative and free source of Harda stone has been located. What is the effect of removing this requirement? (Adding and removing constraints is mentioned in Section 2.3.)

*Answer: $X_1 = 6$, $X_2 = 3$

(c) Example 1 in Chapter 2 solves the quarrying problem with a least-cost objective (instead of least time, as in Chapter 1). The solution indicates that 9 days will be needed to fulfill requirements. How much will it increase costs if quarrying is restricted to 7 days, as suggested in Chapter 2, Example 1.

PROBLEM 3

Three sizes of armor stone A, B, and C are needed for construction of a rubble-mound breakwater. The required tonnages of each are W_A, W_B, and W_C, respectively.

Stone with a unit weight of 165 pounds per cubic foot and of satisfactory quality can be obtained from two potential quarry sites. Field tests indicate that each 1000 cubic yards of rock quarried from site 1 will yield an average 150, 250, and 400 cubic yards of A, B, and C size stone, respectively. Quarrying 1000 cubic yards of rock at site 2 is anticipated to yield 300 cubic yards of each size stone. The remainder at each site would be too small to be useful and would therefore be discarded.

The costs of quarrying at sites 1 and 2 are C_1 and C_2 dollars per 1000 cubic yards of rock, respectively. The costs of hauling and placing in dollars per ton are C_{A1}, C_{B1}, and C_{C1} from site 1 and C_{A2}, C_{B2}, and C_{C2} from site 2. There is neither additional revenue nor cost anticipated from stone quarried at either site but not otherwise utilized.

(a) Formulate a linear programming model which would provide for the needed quantities of stone at least cost.

(b) Revise the previous formulation to account for dredge material which could be used in lieu of (or in addition to) size C stone. The cost of dredging, transporting and placing this material is estimated as C_D dollars per ton.

(c) How can the previous formulations be modified to include set up costs, C_{S1} and C_{S2}, associated with each quarry?

PROBLEM 4

Sue Perfabricator has charge of making frames for windows and doors as needed for a new housing development. A door frame requires about 8 board feet of lumber, 1/4 hour of lathe work, and 1 man-hour for assembly. A window frame requires half as much lumber, 1/3 hour of lathe work, and 2/3 man-hours for assembly.

On a certain day, Sue has available 200 board feet of lumber, 8 hours of lathe time, and 24 man-hours for assembly. What is the maximum number of frames (door and/or window) that can be fabricated? Suppose that at least 18 window frames are needed. How does this affect the maximum number of frames (door and/or window) that can be produced?

PROBLEM 5*

Development in a forested region of a lesser developed country is planned about the ample timber resources there. The pine and fir trees are milled into lumber and plywood using newly constructed mills for each.

Through selective harvesting, an acre of land yields an average of 1.8 million board feet of pine or 1.5 million board feet of fir, depending upon the section of forest. A usable 1000 board feet of lumber requires 2500 board feet of pine or 3000 board feet of fir (or some linear combination). Each 1000 square feet of plywood requires 2000 board feet of either timber.

Prices for lumber have been 225 dollars per thousand board feet, and for plywood 160 dollars per thousand square feet. How should two acres of forest (one acre each of pine and fir) be utilized to yield maximum revenue?

PROBLEM 6

For the lesser developed country of Problem 5, suppose the sawmill has a capacity to handle 60,000 board feet of timber (i.e., pine and/or fir) monthly. The capacity of the plywood mill is 40,000 board feet of timber each month.

(a) Which section(s) of forest should be harvested to maximize monthly revenue? How might the presence of multiple optima be used to advantage?

(b) Suppose a forestry crew working in the pine section can harvest 0.04 acres per month. The same crew can harvest 0.06 acres of fir each month. How should a single forestry crew be deployed to maximize monthly revenue? (Hint: Let a variable, say P, represent the percentage of time the crew spends in the pine section of forest.)

PROBLEM 7

A contractor requires 2000 cubic yards of aggregate for a concrete mix. The aggregate should have a coarse aggregate content less than 25%, intermediate aggregate between 20 and 85%, and fine aggregate between 10 and 20% (all percentages by weight.)

*Answer: Use entire acre of pine (fir) for lumber (plywood); $Z^* = \$282,000$.

Two aggregate sources P and Q are available with the following properties:

	Properties				
	Percent by Weight			Cost	Quantity
Source	Coarse	Intermediate	Fine	($/yd³)	(yd³)
P	10	70	20	12.00	2500
Q	35	50	5	7.50	800

An additional cost of blending a mix of P and Q is estimated as $1.50 per cubic yard of mix.

Determine a least-cost mix of P and/or Q that meets specifications.

PROBLEM 8

A contractor is planning to cap a sheet-pile cofferdam with a soil-cement mixture and has identified three potential borrow areas, A, B, and C. The gradation requirements and characteristics of the three available soils are:

	Percent Passing by Weight			
		Soil Gradations		
Sieve Size	Gradation Requirements	A	B	C
1 inch	97–100%	92	100	100
3/8 inch	86–98%	79	98	100
No. 6	64–90%	50	90	100
No. 50	30–70%	26	34	83
No. 200	10–20%	13	6	35

The costs per cubic yard to excavate, transport, and mix soil are $7.00, $9.00, and $12.00 for soil type A, B, and C, respectively. Formulate (and solve by computer, if available) a linear program to determine the least cost mix.

PROBLEM 9

A painting contractor is seeking a minimum cost blend that meets all specifications for a single coat on a rather large job. Three grades of paint

P_1, P_2, and P_3 and two grades of thinner, T_1 and T_2 are being considered for blending.

There are a number of considerations in forming blends. The viscosity of the blend influences the area per gallon that can be covered. The required surface gloss is achieved by including an additive A in the blend. The color fastness of the paint, that is, its resistance to fading, is enhanced by adding appropriate amounts of a chemical C to the blend. Finally, the vapor pressure of the blend is related to the drying time which should be neither too rapid (later cracking and peeling) nor too slow (prone to imbedded dirt and premature usage). The table lists the characteristics of the prospective blend constituents.

	P_1	P_2	P_3	T_1	T_2
Viscosity (cp)	800	600	400	2	20
Additive A (grams/gal)	20	50	10	0	0
Chemical C (grams/gal)	1500	1000	500	0	0
Vapor pressure (psi)	0.3	0.6	0.9	12.0	8.0
Cost ($/gal)	17.00	15.50	14.20	13.30	12.00

It is reasonable to assume that the constituents blend linearly by volume. Experience indicates that an acceptable blend should have these characteristics:

Viscosity: At least 350 centipoise (cp).

Additive A: Not less than 10 grams/gal nor more than 25 grams/gal.

Chemical C: At least 500 grams /gal.

Vapor pressure: not less than 1 psi nor more than 2 psi.

Use linear programming to determine a minimum cost blend that meets specifications.

(Adapted from G. Hadley, *Linear Programming*, Addison-Wesley, 1962.)

PROBLEM 10

Solve the following problems using the simplex method, the graphic method or the console or hand-held computer, as appropriate.

(a) Minimize: $Z = X_1 + X_2$

such that:
$$X_1 + 5X_2 \geq 25$$
$$2X_1 + X_2 \geq 14$$
$$X_1, X_2 \geq 0$$

(b) Minimize:
$$Z = X_1 + X_2$$

such that:
$$X_1 - 2X_2 \leq 4$$
$$2X_1 + 3X_2 \leq 12$$
$$3X_1 + 4X_2 \geq 12$$
$$X_1, X_2 \geq 0$$

(c) Maximize:
$$Z = 5X_1 - 2X_2$$

such that:
$$2X_1 + X_2 \leq 9$$
$$X_1 - X_2 \leq 2$$
$$-3X_1 + 2X_2 \leq 3$$
$$X_1, X_2 \geq 0$$

(d) Maximize:
$$Z = 2X_1 + 2X_2 - X_3 - X_4$$

such that:
$$2X_1 + X_3 - 2X_4 \leq 6$$
$$2X_1 - 2X_2 - X_3 + X_4 \leq 8$$
$$X_1 + 2X_2 + 2X_4 \leq 7$$
$$X_i \geq 0, \quad i = 1, \ldots, 4$$

(e) Maximize:
$$Z = X_1 + X_2 + X_3 + 2X_4$$

such that:
$$X_1 + X_3 + X_4 \leq 4$$
$$X_1 + X_2 + 2X_4 \leq 8$$
$$X_1 + 2X_2 - X_3 - X_4 \leq 6$$
$$-2X_1 - X_2 + X_3 + 4X_4 \leq 6$$
$$X_i \geq 0, \quad i = 1, \ldots, 4$$

(f) Minimize:
$$Z = X_1 + 3X_2$$

such that:
$$X_1 + 4X_2 \geq 48$$
$$5X_1 + X_2 \geq 50$$
$$X_1, X_2 \geq 0$$

Answers: (a) $X_1 = 5$, $X_2 = 4$; (c) $X_1 = 4$, $X_2 = 2$; (d) $Z^* = 10$, $X_1 = 3$, $X_2 = 2$, $X_3 = X_4 = 0$.

PROBLEM 11

Reconsider Overhill and Dale's problem to alter the terrain of the proposed roadway. Suppose that the cut and fill quantities had been estimated for 500-foot-long sections as indicated in Figure A4.1. Assume that excavation and placement costs are $0.50 and $1.00 per cubic yard, respectively, and that haul costs are only $0.05 per station-yard.

Consider resolving the problem by the mass diagram method. Is the result vastly different from that of the first example?

Formulate the corresponding linear program to minimize earthmoving costs for this revised sectioning scheme. Solve the revised program by computer, if available.

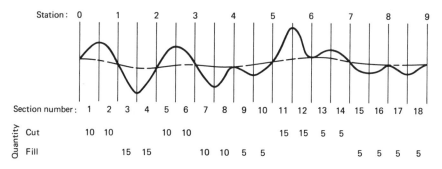

Figure A4.1. Road profile with estimated quantities of cut and fill (in thousand cubic yards).

PROBLEM 12

Review the formulation of a linear program for earthmoving in Chapter 4 and, if available, S. M. Nandgaonkar, "Earthwork Transportation Allocations: Operations Research," *Journal of the Construction Division, American Society of Civil Engineers,* vol. 107, pp. 373–392 (1981). Formulate and solve a numerical problem for earthmoving associated with site grading for a land development project.

PROBLEM 13

Extend Problem 12 to include variable soil characteristics and potential borrow and disposal sites as suggested in Chapter 5.

PROBLEM 14

An asphalt paving contractor has contracted to place bituminous shoulders along an 18-mile roadway and has solicited offers from four property owners to lease sites for his mobile mix plant. Each site's leasing price and distance from one end of the roadway are:

		Site		
	A	B	C	D
Distance (miles)	2	10	12	14
Lease price ($/working day)	20.00	45.00	30.00	50.00
Material transport cost ($/ton)	0.30	0.22	0.20	0.18

The cost of transporting raw material from a convenient rail heading varies with the site location as indicated in the table. The transportation cost of hot mix from plant to roadway is estimated at $0.03 per ton-mile. Each plant relocation, which will be accomplished after normal working hours, will cost $500.00. Finally, the hot mix requirements are 2400 tons per mile while the production capacity of the plant is 800 tons per working day.

Subdivide the roadway into 2-mile increments and formulate a linear program to determine how much mix (if any) should be produced at each potential site. Discuss the advantages and/or disadvantages of increasing/decreasing the length of each roadway subdivision for the formulation.

PROBLEM 15

Quarries $Q1$, $Q2$, and $Q3$ provide material which is processed at plants $P1$ and $P2$ for shipment to construction sites $S1$ and $S2$ (see Figure A4.2).

Let q_1, q_2, and q_3 represent the maximum supplies at $Q1$, $Q2$, and $Q3$ respectively, and s_1 and s_2 the respective needs at $S1$ and $S2$. Unit quarrying and processing costs are c_1, c_2, c_3 and p_1, p_2, respectively. The unit transportation costs from quarry to processing plant are, respectively, t_{11}, t_{12}, t_{21}, t_{22}, t_{31}, and t_{32}. Similarly, unit costs for delivery from processing

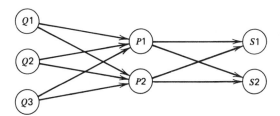

Figure A4.2. Options available for processing and shipping.

plant to construction site are, respectively, d_{11}, d_{12}, d_{21}, and d_{22}. Formulate a linear program to provide the construction needs at minimum cost.

PROBLEM 16

A building contractor has obtained financial backing to enable construction of a maximum 40 custom homes, 90 quality homes, and 60 standard homes. Two large tracts are available. The first, tract A, can accommodate up to 140 homes, while the second, tract B, is adequate for 80 units. The contractor estimates that profits will vary according to the type of home and its location. These estimates are organized into the following table:

	Tract A ($/unit)	Tract B ($/unit)
Custom	4500	5000
Quality	4000	3500
Standard	3500	4500

(a) Formulate a linear program and solve for the mix of homes that maximizes total profit.

(b) Suppose a marketing constraint requires that at least 50% of the homes built on either tract be of the quality type. Revise the previous formulation and solve for the optimal mix of homes.

PROBLEM 17

Separate cost estimates, C_1 and C_2, have been prepared for two jobs being considered for bid. The estimator notes that certain economies could be achieved if both jobs are obtained, that is, the cost of performing both jobs C_{12} is less than the sum of the separate cost estimates. Of course, at this stage one does not know which, if either, of the bids will be successful. How might the chance-weighted-profit function of Chapter 6 be modified to reflect this contingency?

PROBLEM 18

Review Bildenhire's problem in Chapter 6.

(a) When is it a particularly good practice to explore the effect of mesh size?

(b) Resolve Bildenhire's problem for various estimates of the chance-of-winning.

(c) How can the presence of multiple optima be used to good advantage?

PROBLEM 19

A contractor will submit a unit price bid for the site and foundation work indicated in the following table.

Work Item	Unit	Estimated Quantity Proposal	Estimated Quantity Contractor's	Normal Unit Price ($)
Clear and grub	yds^2	450	450	3.50
Earth excavation	yds^3	1100	1200	24.00
Rock excavation	yds^3	300	200	44.00
Foundation piles	lin. ft.	3200	3600	8.00
Pile caps	ea.	10	10	650.00
Landscaping	yds^2	450	420	5.00

The contractor has decided upon a total bid of $79,500 considering the competition and the differences between his quantity estimates and those of the proposal. Formulate and solve a linear program to determine how the contractor should unbalance his bid without raising or lowering his normal unit prices by more than 20%.

PROBLEM 20

A unit price proposal for modernization and improvement of an existing port facility is shown below.

Item	Description	Unit	Quantity (estimated)	Unit Price	Item Total
1	Removal: Existing structures	lump sum	1		
2	Dredging	yds^3	74,000		
3	Bulkhead: Fill	yds^3	34,000		
4	Bulkhead: Sheet piling	lineal feet	24,500		
5	Pier: Concrete piling	lineal feet	62,000		
6	Pier: Case-in-place concrete	yds^3	18,800		
7	Pier: Appurtenances	lump sum	1		
8	Utilities: Water/Elec	lump sum	1		
			Bid total =		_____

After reviewing the project and assessing the potential competition, one bidder desires to submit a bid of $6,980,000. Given this bidder's quantity estimates, anticipated construction schedule, and allowable range of unit prices as shown in the table which follows, formulate a linear program to maximize the present worth of revenue. Assume the bidder, if successful, will be paid in full at the end of each year for work in place and that a 15% annual interest rate is appropriate for discounting.

| Item | Quantity Estimates | Bidder's Construction Schedule | | | Range of Unit Prices |
		Year 1	Year 2	Year 3	
1	1 (lump sum)	1			$240,000–280,000
2	78,000 (yds^3)	30,000	20,000	8,000	$8.00–9.20
3	33,500 (yds^3)		24,000	9,500	$9.00–12.00
4	26,000 (ft)		26,000		$13.00–15.00
5	66,000 (ft)		22,000	44,000	$48.00–66.00
6	18,800 (yds^3)			18,000	$78.00–94.00
7	1 (lump sum)		0.2	0.8	$38,000–54,000
8	1 (lump sum)			1	$60,000–90,000

PROBLEM 21

A contractor is to build a bridge that spans east-west across a river and requires two pile-supported abutments on the river banks. The work activities, anticipated durations, and precedence relationships associated with constructing the abutments are as follows:

Task	Description	Duration (days)	Preceding Tasks
A	Clear site, E-bank	10	—
B	Clear site, W-bank	8	A
C	Set up casting yard	3	A
D	Deliver materials	1	C
E	Cast and cure piles	15	D
F	Excavation, E-bank	4	B
G	Excavation, W-bank	4	F
H	Drive piles, E-bank	3	E,F
I	Stage piles, W-bank	1	E,G
J	Drive piles, W-bank	3	H,I
K	Place formwork/rebar, E-bank	4	H

Task	Description	Duration (days)	Preceding Tasks
L	Place formwork/rebar, W-bank	3	J, K
M	Pour concrete and cure	15	K, L
N	Set steel framework, E-bank	2	M
P	Set steel framework, W-bank	1	N, R
Q	Backfill, E-bank	2	N, R
R	Backfill, W-bank	2	M

Formulate the corresponding linear program to determine the minimum time to complete this phase of bridge construction. If a computer is available, solve this program and compare the solution with the (manual) critical path method suggested in Chapter 8.

PROBLEM 22*

The costs, durations, and precedence data for a construction project consisting of 6 activities, A through F, are as follows:

Task	Normal Conditions Cost ($000)	Normal Conditions Time (days)	Crash Conditions Cost ($000)	Crash Conditions Time (days)	Preceding Tasks
A	12	9	21	7	—
B	8	8	10	6	A
C	18	6	20	5	A
D	12	8	24	4	B
E	8	12	18	8	C
F	9	9	12	7	D, E

(a) Formulate a linear program to determine the least cost schedule if the project must be completed in 30 days. Solve this linear program if a computer is available. (Assume the increase in cost for each crash effort is directly proportional to the time saved.)

(b) Suppose a bonus of $5000 has been offered for each day the project is completed ahead of day 30. Revise and solve, if possible, the previous linear program to determine the optimal completion time.

*Answers: (a) $82,500; (b) 28 days.

PROBLEM 23

Solve the contractor's trim-loss problem in section A1.7.

PROBLEM 24

To enhance employment opportunities and to provide a continuing supply
of skilled personnel, a 5-year Building Industry Advancement Program
is planned.

Two training courses are to be offered: one to last 1 year and the other
for 2 years. Bonuses B_{1t} and B_{2t} are planned to encourage enrollment in
each course commencing in year t for $t = 1, 2, 3, 4$ and 5. Enrollment goals
for the total numbers in training in each year have been established as N_1,
N_2, N_3, N_4, and N_5.

(a) Let X_{1t} and X_{2t} be the numbers enrolled in each course beginning in
     year t. Formulate a linear programming model to guide an optimal
     (minimum bonus) recruitment policy.

(b) Suppose the total numbers of graduates desired at the end of each
     training year are M_1, M_2, M_3, M_4 and M_5. Modify the previous formu-
     lation for graduation needs assuming all trainees will graduate in
     their designated years.

APPENDIX 5

ADDITIONAL READING

The linear optimization literature is varied and vast. Here is a sampling, any of which will be a source for additional references:

S. I. Gass, *Linear Programming: Methods and Applications,* 4th edition, McGraw-Hill, New York (1975).

G. Hadley, *Linear Programming,* Addison-Wesley, Reading, Mass. (1962).

A readable introduction to linear programming is provided by:

A. M. Glicksman, *Linear Programming and the Theory of Games,* John Wiley, New York (1963).

Replete with imaginative uses of linear programming with ample exercises to develop skills are either of the two editions of:

H. M. Wagner, *Principles of Operations Research: With Applications to Managerial Decisions,* Prentice-Hall, Englewood Cliffs, N. J. (1969, 1975).

The diversity of linear programming applications is indicated in an IBM publication:

A Preface to Linear Programming and Its Applications (1970).

Among several titles on quantitative construction management that include some discussions of linear programming and applications are:

J. J. Adrian, *Quantitative Methods in Construction Management,* American Elsevier, New York (1973).

R. J. Aguilar, *Systems Analysis and Design in Engineering, Architecture, Construction, and Planning,* Prentice-Hall, Englewood Cliffs, N. J. (1973).

R. Pilcher, *Principles of Construction Management,* 2nd edition, McGraw-Hill, London (1976).

M. Varma, *Systems Techniques in Construction Management,* Metropolitan Publishing Co., New Delhi (1979).

Some chapters on linear optimization with civil engineering applications appear in:

R. M. Stark and R. L. Nicholls, *Mathematical Foundations for Design: Civil Engineering Systems,* McGraw-Hill, New York (1972).

References relevant to individual chapters are as follows:

Chapters 1 and 2

Additional examples of a similar nature appear in Stark and Nicholls and in Wagner.

Chapter 3

The following suggest linear programming for aggregate blending:

C. B. Manula and H. Gezik, "Applications of Linear Programming in the Crushed Stone Industry," Department of Mining, Pennsylvania State University, University Park, Pa. (Sept. 1967).

J. B. Ritter and L. R. Shaffer, "Blending Natural Earth Deposits for Least Cost," *Journal of the Construction Division, American Society of Civil Engineers,* vol. 87, pp. 39–62 (1961).

Chapters 4 and 5

The source for much of these chapters was:

R. H. Mayer, Jr. and R. M. Stark, "Earthmoving Logistics," *Journal of the Construction Division, American Society of Civil Engineers,* vol. 107, pp. 297–312 (1981).

A discussion of the mass diagram and other topics for earthwork logistics appears in several texts including these two:

J. C. L. Fish, *Earthwork Haul and Overhaul,* John Wiley, New York (1913).

C. H. Ogelsby, *Highway Engineering,* 3rd edition, John Wiley, New York (1975).

Chapter 6

A number of illustrative examples concerning capital budgeting and linear programming under conditions of uncertainty are provided in Aguilar and in Wagner. An extended discussion of capital budgeting appears in:

H. M. Weingartner, *Mathematical Programming and the Analysis of Capital Budgeting Problems,* Prentice-Hall, Englewood Cliffs, N. J. (1963).

Chapter 7

The source for much of this chapter was:

R. M. Stark, "Unbalanced Highway Contract Tendering," *Operational Research Quarterly,* vol. 25, pp. 373–388 (1974).

The unbalancing of bids as well as other aspects of contract bidding are discussed in:

J. E. Diekmann, R. H. Mayer, Jr., and R. M. Stark, "Coping with Uncertainty in Unit Price Contracting," *Journal of the Construction Division, American Society of Civil Engineers,* vol. 108, pp. 379–389 (1982).

M. Gates, "Bidding Strategies and Probabilities," *Journal of the Construction Division, American Society of Civil Engineers,* vol. 93, pp. 75–107 (1967).

Chapter 8

The critical path literature is extensive. Two titles are:

L. R. Shaffer, J. B. Ritter, and W. L. Meyer, *The Critical Path Method,* McGraw-Hill, New York (1965).

R. W. Woodhead and J. Antill, *Critical Path Methods in Construction Practice,* 2nd edition, Wiley-Interscience, New York (1970).

Linear approximations to certain nonlinear terms and equations are discussed in Stark and Nicholls and in Wagner.

INDEX